THE ULTIMATE BATHROOM JOKE BOOK

THE ULTIMATE BATHROOM JOKE BOOK

QUICK-WITTED QUICK READING TO PASS THE TIME ON THE POTTY

Edited by Marcia Kamien

Cover by Carol Russo Design

Platinum Press, LLC
2013

Copyright 2013 by Platinum Press, LLC

All rights reserved. No part of this publication may be reproduced, stored in a retrieval system, or transmitted in any form, or by any means, electronic, photocopying, recording, or otherwise, without written permission from the publisher.

ISBN #978-1-879582-77-4

Printed and bound in the United States of America

First Edition

987654321

CONTENTS

Short and Snappy 1

Age before Beauty……………….59

Puns and Games 103

Wit and Wisdom 133

Kids and More Kids 213

This and That 257

Signs and Slogans 327

Short and Sassy 351

The Ultimate Bathroom Joke Book

SHORT AND SNAPPY

I didn't make it to the gym today. That makes five years.

A penny saved is a government oversight.

Pessimist: the glass is half empty
Optimist: the glass if half full
Me: Yay! There's room to add vodka!

You can't buy happiness but you can buy cupcakes and that's sort of the same thing.

The greatest pleasure in life is doing what people have told you can't be done.

I'm not an alcoholic. Alcoholics go to meetings. I'm a drunk; we go to parties.

At my age, I need glasses: glasses of wine, glasses of beer, glasses of scotch, and so forth.

If I told you where the self-help section is…that would kind of defeat the purpose, now, wouldn't it?

Macho doesn't prove mucho.

A dyslexic man walked into a bra.

Life is like a roll of toilet paper. The closer it gets to the end, the faster it goes.

I love Christmas lights. They remind me of Democrat, Republican and Independent politicians. They all hang together, half of them don't work, and the ones that do aren't all that bright.

You do not need a parachute to skydive. You only need a parachute to skydive twice.

Woody Allen said: I don't want to become immortal through my work. I want to become immortal through not dying.

Many people are alive only because it's illegal to shoot them.

We childproofed our house…but they get in anyway.

Get married? I can't mate in captivity.

I chose the road less traveled. Now where the hell am I?

In filling out an application, where it says "in case of emergency, notify" I put DOCTOR.

Never buy a car you can't push.

WARNING: the consumption of alcohol may cause you to tell friends over and over that you love them.

Grandchildren are God's reward for not killing your children.

I just got off the phone with a friend living in Canada. He said that since early this morning the snow has been nearly waist high and is still falling. His wife has been looking through the window, just staring. He says that if it gets much worse, he may have to let her in.

Deja Moo: the feeling you've heard this bull.

You're never too old to learn something stupid.

Save the Earth! It's the only planet with chocolate!

I've learned so much from making mistakes, I'm thinking of making a few more.

How can there be self-help groups?

Mother: You're 30, all your friends are married. You should be married.
Daughter: You're 65, all your friends have hip replacements. You should get a hip replacement.

Did you know that when a woman wears a leather dress, a man's heart beats faster, his throat gets dry, he gets weak in the knees, and he can hardly think straight? Yes! Because she smells like a new truck!

Southerners know the difference between a hissie fit and a conniption fit. They also know that you don't "have" them, you "pitch" them.

Ask me about my third chromosome.

How the hell are you supposed to fold a fitted sheet?

Clarence Darrow said: When I was a boy I was told that anyone could become President. I'm beginning to believe it.

I don't believe it. I failed my urine test.

Men wake up as handsome as they were when they went to sleep.
Women somehow deteriorate during the night.

A fool and his money are soon elected.

Going to McDonald's for a salad is like going to a whore for a hug.

If you were to spell out numbers (one, two, three, etc.) how far would you have to go before you used the letter 'a?'
1,000.

I always cook with wine. Sometimes I even put it in the food.

It's not easy being a mother. If it were easy, fathers would do it.

Why aren't there any B batteries?

Long ago, when men cursed and beat the ground with sticks, it was called witchcraft. Today, we call it golf.

WHY MEN ARE SELDOM DEPRESSED

- Your name is yours for life.
- The garage is all yours.
- Wedding plans take care of themselves
- Car mechanics tell you the truth.
- You can be President.
- The world is your urinal.
- You don't have to stop and think which way to turn the nut on a bolt.
- Wrinkles add character
- Same work, more pay.
- People never stare at your chest when you're talking to them.
- New shoes never cut, blister or mangle your feet.
- The same hairstyle lasts for years, maybe decades.
- You know stuff about tanks.
- You can play with toys your whole life.
- 3 pairs of shoes are quite enough.
- You can "do" your nails with a pocketknife.
- You will never get pregnant.
- The wrinkles in your face add character.
- You don't realize your clothes need cleaning.
- You'll probably never dye your hair.

Hospitality is making your guests feel at home. Even if you wish they really were.

Some people cause happiness wherever they go, others whenever they go.

Why is it that one careless match can start a forest fire, but it takes a whole box of them to start a campfire?

A clear conscience is a sign of a bad memory.

WARNING: the consumption of alcohol may cause you to think you can sing.

Sometimes I'll check my watch three consecutive times... and still not know what time it is.

How many times must one say "What?" before just nodding and smiling as if you understood.

I love the feeling of camaraderie when an entire line of cars team up to prevent a jerk from greasing in from the front. Stay strong, brothers and sisters!

Never despair. But if you do, carry on in despair.

OLD is when a sexy babe or hunk catches your eye and your pacemaker opens the garage door.

The first testicular guard, the "cup", was used in hockey in 1874; and the first helmet was used in 1974. That means it only took 100 years for men to realize that their brain is also important.

Nothing sucks more than that moment during an argument when you realize you're wrong.

The state with the highest percentage of people who walk to work? Alaska!

The percentage of Africa that's wilderness: 28%. The percentage of North America that's wilderness: 38%.

A man should forget his mistakes. No use in two people remembering the same thing!

I'm speeding because I have to get there before I forget where I'm going.

Men think that every girl's dream is to find the perfect man. Not so. Every girl's dream is to be able to eat anything and not get fat.

WARNING: the consumption of alcohol may cause you to think you're whispering when you're NOT.

Dolphins are so smart, that within a few weeks of captivity, they can train grown people to stand on the edge of the pool and throw fish to them.

A salesman rings a doorbell and the door is answered by a small boy who has a lighted cigar in one hand and a glass of whisky in the other. The man says, "Hello, there sonny, is your Mom or Dad home?" "What the hell do you think???"

I pointed to two old drunks sitting across the bar from us and said to my friend, "That's us in ten years."
He said, "Dummy, that's a mirror!"

Will Rogers famously said: If we got one-tenth of what's promised to us in these acceptance speeches, there wouldn't be any reason to go to Heaven.

The way I look at it, if the children are still alive when my husband gets home from work...I've done my job.

This country is run by men. Need I say more?

I recently became a Christian Scientist. It was the only health plan I could afford.

My reality check just bounced.

When we talk to God, we're praying. When God talks to us, we're schizophrenic.

I was street smart. Unfortunately, the street was Rodeo Drive. -Carrie Fisher

Boxing is like ballet, except that there's no music, no choreography, and the dancers hit each other.

Television has proved that people will watch anything rather than look at each other.

My children refused to eat anything that hadn't danced on TV.
                              -Erma Bombeck

A seminar on time travel will be held two weeks ago.

All those who don't agree, signify by saying "I resign."

I've been on a calendar but never on time.
                                      -Marilyn Monroe

The day after tomorrow is the third day of the rest of your life.

What's a "free" gift? Aren't all gifts free?

You'll go to Heck if you don't believe in Gosh.

WARNING: the consumption of alcohol may cause pregnancy.

The trouble with unwritten rules is they're so difficult to erase.

Freedom is just chaos with better lighting.

New clinical studies show there are no answers.

Gravity isn't my fault. I voted for Velcro.

A woman is a woman until the day she dies, but a man's a man only as long as he can.
-Moms Mabley

If you can smile when things go wrong, you have someone else to blame.

I don't buy temporary insanity as a murder defense. Breaking into someone's house and ironing all their clothes: <u>that's</u> temporary insanity.

I read this article. It said the typical symptoms of stress are eating too much, drinking too much, impulse buying, and driving too fast. Are they kidding? This is my idea of a great day!
-Monica Piper

I'm a vegetarian not because I love animals but because I hate plants.

Cricket is basically baseball on Valium.

You can name your salary here. I named mine Zelda.

Adults are always asking little kids what they want to be when they grow up because they're looking for ideas.
                              -Paula Poundstone

Monogamy leaves a lot to be desired.

The problem with trouble-shooting is that trouble shoots back.

There are very few jobs that actually require a penis or a vagina. All other jobs should be open to everyone.

Talk is cheap. Until you hire a lawyer.

I'm not your type. I have a pulse.

Ask your child what he wants for dinner only if he's buying.
                              -Fran Lebowitz

I want to have children while my parents are still young enough to take care of them.

If you don't take care of your body, where will you live?

On a t-shirt: Two wrongs are only the beginning.

When I was a little girl, I had only two friends and they were imaginary. And they would play only with each other.
                              -Rita Rudner

I've figured out why first dates don't work so well. It's because they usually take place in a restaurant. Women are weird and confused and unhappy about food; and men are weird and confused and unhappy about money...yet off they go, the minute they meet, to where you use money to buy food.
                              –Adair Lara

My heart is as pure as the driven slush.
                              -Tallulah Bankhead

It's so beautifully arranged on the plate. You just know someone's fingers have been all over it.   -Julia Child

Too much of a good thing can be wonderful.
                              - Mae West

Instant gratification takes too long.
                              -Carrie Fisher

I figure you have the same chance of winning the lottery whether you play or not.
                              -Fran Lebowitz

I'll wear any color as long as it's black.

A child develops individuality long before he develops taste. I have seen my kid straggle into the kitchen in the morning wearing outfits that need only one accessory: an empty gin bottle.
                              -Erma Bombeck

Eternal nothingness is okay if you're dressed for it.

My grandmother was a very tough woman. She buried three husbands and two of them were only napping.
                              -Rita Rudner

There is no heaven or hell. There is only smoking and non-smoking.

I had amnesia once...or maybe twice.

I got this powdered water...now I don't know what to add.   -Steven Wright

The Ultimate Bathroom Joke Book

What do hippy horses say? Hay, man.

A fine is a tax for doing wrong. A tax is a fine for doing well.

Those who live by the sword get shot by those who don't.

Eve must have been Jewish. Who else would have said to an amorous guy, "Here, have a piece of fruit."

I blame my mother for my poor sex life. All she told me was, "The man goes on top and the woman goes underneath." For years, my husband and I slept in bunk beds.
                                        -Joan Rivers

Ah, yes, divorce ... from the Latin word meaning to rip out a man's genitals through his wallet.   –Robin Williams

Health: what my friends are always drinking to, just before they fall down.   -Phyllis Diller

WARNING: the consumption of alcohol may cause you to act like a lunatic.

He who laughs last, thinks slowest.

ACTUAL REAL-LIFE NEWSPAPER HEADLINES

Worker suffers leg pain after crane drops 800-pound ball on his head

Study Shows Frequent Sex Enhances Pregnancy Chances

City unsure why the sewer smells

Bridges help people cross rivers

Meeting on open meetings is closed

Homicide victims rarely talk to police

Man Accused of Killing Lawyer Receives a New Attorney

County to pay $250,000 to advertise lack of funds

Statistics show that teen pregnancy drops off significantly after age 25.

Man with 8 DUIs blames drinking problem

Immortality is a long shot, I admit. But somebody has to be first.   -Bill Cosby

The President of today is just the postage stamp of tomorrow.   -Gracie Allen

I got a chain letter by fax. It's simple. You just fax a dollar bill to everybody on the list.
     –Steven Wright

Did you ever stop to realize that wrong numbers are never busy?

It's said that if you lined up all the cars in the world end to end, someone from California would be stupid enough to try to pass them all.

THE 50-50-90 RULE: Any time you have a 50-50 chance of getting something right, there's a 90% probability you'll get it wrong.

If the shoe fits, get another one just like it.

He who hesitates is probably right.

A man doesn't understand women twice in his life. Before marriage and after marriage.

I never pay my bills. I have the money, but I'm lonely and I want someone to call me.

My wife is too neat. I get up at 3 in the morning for a drink of water and by the time I get back, she's made the bed!

Gambling is a great way of getting nothing for something.
The suspicious husband calls home and asks the trusted housekeeper, "Where is my wife?" "She's in bed with her lover."
Husband says, "This is an order. Get the rifle from the gun cabinet, shoot them both, and return to the phone. I'll hold."
The housekeeper returns and says, "Done."
"Good. Throw them both into the swimming pool."
"But, sir, we have no swimming pool."
After a beat: "What phone number is this?"

If it's the Psychic Network, why do they need a phone number?

The things that come to those who wait may well be the things left by those who got there first.

ROBIN WILLIAMS, VERY FUNNY MAN

I like my wine like my women—ready to pass out.

Carpe per diem: seize the check.

Do you think God gets stoned? I think so ... just look at the platypus.

Gentiles are people who eat mayonnaise for no reason.

Comedy is acting out optimism.

Reality is just a crutch for people who can't deal with drugs.

See, the problem is that God gives men a brain and a penis and only enough blood to run one at a time.

Reality. What a concept!

Spring is Nature's way of saying, "Let's party!"

A blonde spots a letter lying on her doormat. It says DO NOT BEND and she spends the next few hours trying to figure out how to get it.

You're not fat. You're just easy to see.

People think I'm quiet because I'm shy; but really, I've been silently judging them from afar and I have determined that they're all retards.

I hope this poem has the same effect on you as it did on me. Then it will have been worth forwarding to you. Imagine we are walking on a country road, birds singing in the trees, and hearing this beautiful poem about growing old . . .
Damn, I forgot the words!

For our 25th anniversary, my wife and I went back to the hotel where we spent our wedding night...only this time, I stayed in the bathroom and cried.

Cogito ergo spud. I think, therefore I yam.

Five days a week, my body is a temple. The other two days, it's an amusement park.

You are not drunk if you can lie on the floor without holding on.

Forgive your enemy, but remember the bastard's name.

In a scene from The Crossing Guard: Bartender to Jack Nicholson: "These guys came out of the men's room, arguing... in Japanese I think. So I said to them, 'Listen, fellas, this is America. Speak Spanish!'"

A blonde is in jail. A guard looks in and sees her hanging by her feet.
"What the hell are you doing?" he demands.
"Hanging myself," she replies.
"It should be around your neck," the guard says.
"I know," she replies, "But I couldn't breathe."

My wife has been missing for a week now. The police said to prepare for the worst. So I had to go down to Good Will to get back all of her clothes.

If a vegetarian eats only vegetables, then what does a humanitarian eat?

Just been to the gym. They've got a new machine. Could only use it for half an hour, as I started to feel sick. It's great, though. Provides me with everything I need: KitKats, Mars Bars, Snickers, potato chips...

If God wanted us to vote, he would have given us candidates.   -Jay Leno

I no longer prepare food with more than one ingredient.   -Cyra McFadden

Divorce is expensive because it's worth it.

Why pay money to have your family tree traced? Go into politics and your opponents will do it for you.

I was probably the only revolutionary referred to as cute.   -Abbie Hoffman

I went to San Francisco. I found someone's heart. Now what?

Teach a child to be polite and courteous in the home and, when he grows up, he'll never be able to merge his car into the highway traffic.

My weight is perfect for my height—which varies.

Is it me—or do Buffalo wings taste just like chicken?

Show me a man with both feet firmly on the ground and I'll show you a man who can't get his pants off.

If you can smile when things go wrong, you must have someone else to blame.

Old cooks never die, they just get deranged.

A bus station is where a bus stops. A train station is where a train stops. I have a work station.

The last thing I want to do is hurt you. But it's still on my list.

I said No to drugs; but they didn't listen.

NEW MEDICAL DEFINITIONS

Artery….the study of paintings
Bacteria…back door to the cafeteria
CatScan….searching for kitty
Cauterize…made eye contact with
D & C….where Washington is
Dilate…to live a long life
G.I. Series…world series of military baseball
Hangnail…where you put your coat
Impotent…distinguished, well known
Labor pain… getting hurt at work
Morbid…higher than I bid
Outpatient…a person who has fainted
Recovery Room…a place to do upholstery
Rectum…damn near killed him
Secretion…hiding something
Terminal illness….getting sick at the airport
Tumor…more than one
Urine…opposite of you're out

We all need to go sometime. Why don't you go now?

War doesn't determine who is right … only who is left.

Life is a glorious cycle of song,
A medley of extemporania.
And love is a thing that can never go wrong,
And I am Marie of Rumania.
                              -Dorothy Parker

New clinical studies show there are no answers.

Asking if computers can think is like asking if submarines can swim.

Do not argue with an idiot. He will drag you down to his level and beat you with experience.

The problem with political jokes is they get elected.

Those who are too smart to engage in politics are punished by being governed by those who are dumber.

Nostalgia isn't what it used to be.

Always question authority. Ask me anything.

A verbal contract isn't worth the paper it's written on.   -Sam Goldwyn

Don't let your mind wander. It's too little to be allowed out alone.

Q: Why is the track at the Indy 500 an oval?
A: So men won't have to stop and ask directions.

If space and time are curved, then where do all the straight people come from?

Basically, my husband has two beliefs in life. He believes in God and he believes that when the gas gauge is on empty, he still has a quarter of a tank.
He thinks the "E" stands for "Ehhh, there's still some left."   -Rita Rudner

Always read books that will make you look good if you die in the middle.

My father never lived to see his dream come true of an all-Yiddish-speaking Canada.
                              -David Steinberg

Old investors never die, they just roll over.

Birthdays are good for you. The more you have, the longer you live.

Finally, a computer setting I can understand:
"Windows cannot find that file. Would you like some white wine instead?"

Someone told me they make ice cubes out of leftover wine. This is confusing. Just what is leftover wine?

You know someone's from the South because they grow up knowing the difference between "right near" and "a right far piece." They also know that "just down the road" can be one mile or twenty.

Speaking of the South, here's a grammar lesson:
Y'all is singular, all y'all is plural. "Fixin'" is a word that can be used as a noun, a verb, or an adverb.
If you can't be kind, at least have the decency to be vague.

When everything's coming your way, you are in the wrong lane.

Explain to me again why I shouldn't eat my young.

Women will never be equal with men until they can walk down the street with a bald head and beer gut and think they're sexy.

WARNING: the consumption of alcohol may create the illusion that you are tougher, smarter, faster and better-looking than most people.

Guy goes to the doctor. The doctor sees he has a frog on his head.
Doctor: How can I help you?
Frog: Can you get this guy off my behind?

In the old days in Soviet Russia, collective farms were expected to meet certain crop limits. A commissar came to one such farm and asked about production.
Worker: "The potatoes are piled as high as the knee of God."
Commissar: "There is no God."
Worker: "There are no potatoes."

Mark Twain said it.
 "I thoroughly disapprove of duels. If a man should challenge me, I would take him kindly by the hand and lead him to a quiet place and kill him."

The drunk was showing off his new place. In the bedroom was a huge gong, which he called his talking clock. His friends said they didn't see how a gong could be a clock, not to mention a talking one.
"It talks," he said. "I'll prove it." He gave the gong a big whack which of course created a very loud reverberating sound. From the other side of the wall came a voice:
"You idiot! Don't you know it's 2:00 AM?"

Boxing is like ballet, except that there's no music, no choreography and the dancers hit each other.

LA police had a lineup. They asked each man to repeat the words "Give me all your money or I'll shoot!" At which one man shouted, "That's not what I said!"
Case closed.

Marriage is like a deck of cards.
In the beginning all you need are two hearts and a diamond.
By the end, you wish you had a club and a spade.

LIFE BEFORE THE COMPUTER
Memory was something you lost with age.
A program was a TV show.
An application was for employment.
A cursor used profanity.
A keyboard was a piano.
A web was a spider's home.
A CD was a bank account.
A hard drive was a long trip on the road.
A mouse pad was where a mouse lived.
And if you had a 3 ½ floppy, you just hoped that nobody ever found out.

World's Shortest Books
THINGS I CANNOT AFFORD by Bill Gates
LIVING LIFE TO ITS FULLEST by Jack Kevorkian
TO ALL THE MEN WE HAVE LOVED BEFORE by Rosie O'Donnell and Ellen de Generes.
OUR WHITE BOYFRIENDS by the Kardashians
MY BLACK GIRLFRIENDS by Tiger Woods
THE AMISH PHONE DIRECTORY
DATING ETIQUETTE by Mike Tyson
MY PLAN TO FIND THE REAL KILLER by O.J. Simpson and Casey Anthony.

A man in Brooklyn, pretending to have a gun, kidnapped a motorist and forced him to drive to two different automated bank machines. Whereupon the kidnapper proceeded to withdraw money from his own bank account.
He couldn't afford a cab?

I cook using the four food groups:
CANNED .BOXED .BAGGED .FROZEN

Rise? If I must. But shine?
That ain't happening!

A farmer borrows money from the bank to buy a bull to service his cows; but it turns out the bull is just not interested.
The banker finds a vet for the farmer and then goes to the farm to see how things are going.
The famer says: "What a great vet! That bull has serviced all my cows and all the neighbors' cows, too."
"What did the vet do?" asks the banker.
"Just gave him some pills," the farmer says.
"What kind?" asks the banker.
"Dunno, but they sort of taste like mint."
My life is based on a true story.

A man is a person who, if a woman says, "Never mind, I'll do it myself"...lets her.
A woman is a person who, if she says to a man, "Never mind, I'll do it myself" and he lets her...gets mad.
A man is a person who, if a woman says she'll do it herself and he lets her and she gets mad...says "What are you so mad about?"
A woman is a person who, if she says she'll do it herself and he lets her and then wants to know why she's mad...says, "If you don't know, I'm not going to tell you."

A teenager lost a contact lens while playing hoops in the driveway. After searching, he told his mother it was gone for good.
Undaunted, she went outside and returned soon with the lens.
"How did you manage that, Mom?" he asked.
"Well," she explained, "You were looking for a small piece of plastic, whereas I was looking for $150."

Marriage means commitment.
Of course, so does insanity.

An Indian chief was asked by his son, "How did you name my sister?"
The chief answered, "When she was conceived, dawn was about to break. So we named her Rising Sun.
Why do you ask, Broken Condom?"

Gross ignorance: 144 times worse than ignorance.

A mob boss gives his son a gun on his 16th birthday.
The boy swaps the gun for a beautiful watch. His father is disgusted. "You are a dum-dum, you know that? Ten years from now, you're married and you come home early to find your wife in bed with another man. What are you gonna do? Look at your watch and say, "It's late, time to go home?"

Gravity: not just a good idea. It's a law!

Cynic: someone who smells the flowers and looks for the casket.

My mother was 88 years old and didn't need glasses. Drank right out of the bottle.
–Henny Youngman

GONE BUT NOT FORGOT: George Carlin

Should vegetarians eat animal crackers?

If the cops arrest a mime, do they tell him he has the right to remain silent?

Why don't sheep shrink when it rains?

Is it possible to be totally partial?

If a parsley farmer is sued, can they garnish his wages?

Where do forest rangers go, to get away from it all?

When sign makers go on strike, is anything written on their signs?

If, instead of talking to your plants, you yelled at them, would they grow only to be troubled and insecure?

If a stealth bomber crashes, will it make a sound?

Strangers have the best candy.

If a turtle loses its shell, is it naked or homeless?

The hit-and-run victim was just struggling to his feet when a policeman ran up to help.
"My mother-in-law just tried to run me over!" the shaken man told the cop.
"You were hit from behind. How do you know who it was?" asked the officer.
"I recognized her laugh."

When a physician remarked on the new patient's ruddy complexion, the man said, "It's high blood pressure, Doc. It comes from my family."
"Your mother's side, or your father's?"
"Neither," said the patient. "It's from my wife's family."
"Oh come now," said the doctor. "You couldn't possibly get your high pressure from her family."
"You should meet her mother, Doc."

It's possible blondes also prefer gentlemen.

A procrastinator's job is never done.

When God sneezed, I didn't know what to say.

FUNNY LINES FROM ACTUAL MEDICAL CHARTS

*The patient has been depressed since she started seeing me three years ago.

*Skin: somewhat pale, but present.

*Patient has two teenaged children but no other abnormalities.

*Patient was alert and unresponsive.

*Patient is numb from her toes down.

*Occasional, constant, infrequent headaches.

*Patient had waffles for breakfast and anorexia for lunch.

*While in the ER, he was examined, X-rated and sent home.

*The patient refused an autopsy.

*Discharge status: alive but without permission.

A WOMAN'S DICTIONARY

Blonde jokes: Jokes that are short so men can understand them.

Hardware store: Similar to a black hole in space. If he goes in, he isn't coming out any time soon.

Zillion: The number of times you ask a man to do something he doesn't feel like doing, so you end up doing it yourself.

Patience: The most important ingredient for dating, marriage and children. See also "tranquillizers."

Eternity: the last two minutes of a football game.

Cooking on the Grill: You bought the groceries, trimmed the meat, washed and cut the salad, poked holes in the potatoes and cleaned up. But he "made dinner."

Park: before children, meaning to go somewhere romantic...after children, meaning a place with swings and slides.

Thus the metric system did not really catch on in the United States—unless you count the increasing popularity of the nine-millimeter bullet.

–Dave Barry

I know there are people who do not love their fellow man and I hate people like that!

-Tom Lehrer

If you don't attend the funerals of your friends, they will certainly not attend yours.

-H.L. Menken

I told the doctor I broke my leg in two places. He told me to stop going to those places.

–Henny Youngman

The reason there are two Senators for each state is so that one can be the designated driver.

–Jay Leno

Teenagers, remember that you are in the last stage of your life in which you will be happy to hear that the phone is for you.

-Fran Lebowitz

GETTING THE LAST, HUMOROUS, WORD

On the gravestone of John Penny:
  Reader if cash thou art in want of any
  Dig 4 feet deep and thou wilt find a Penny.

In a Maryland cemetery:
  Here lies an atheist
  All dressed up and no place to go.

On a grave in Richmond, Virginia:
  She always said her feet were killing her
  But nobody believed her.

On a plain unembellished stone:
  I was somebody.
  Who, is no business of yours.

In Nova Scotia:
  Here lies Ezekiel Aikle Age 102
  The Good Die Young

And in New Mexico: Here lies Johnny Yeast
  Pardon me for not rising.

On a gravestone in Troy, New York:
  I told you I was sick!

On the one hand, we'll never experience childbirth. On the other, we can open our own jars.
>   –Bruce Willis

Luge strategy? Lie flat and try not to die.
>   –Carmen Boyle,
>   Olympic Luge Gold Medal winner

I read somewhere that 77 percent of all the mentally ill live in poverty. Actually, I'm more intrigued by the 23 percent who are apparently doing quite well.
>   -Jerry Garcia, Grateful Dead

My cousin just died. He got stung by a bee, the natural enemy of a tightrope walker.
>   -Dan Rather

There are only two reasons to sit at the back of a plane: either you have diarrhea or you're eager to meet people who do.
>   -Henry Kissinger

Gary Cooper and Greta Garbo may actually be the same person. Have you ever seen them together?
>   -Ernst Lubitsch

Old hippies never die; they just smell that way.

Thomas Jefferson's slaves loved him so much, they called him by a special name: Dad.
         –Mark Russell

Ever notice that irons have a setting for Permanent Press? I don't get it.
         -Steven Wright

I took my Biology exam last Friday.
I was asked to name two things commonly found in cells.
Apparently "blacks" and "Roumanian gypsies" were not the correct answers.

A plump girl served me at McDonald's when it was very crowded. "Sorry about the wait," she said. I said, "Don't worry, dear, you'll lose it eventually."

A man goes to his bank manager and says, "I'd like to start a small business. How do I go about it?"
The manager says, "Start a big one and wait."

Karaoke: a Japanese word meaning "tone deaf."

Normal: a setting on the washing machine.

Sleep: that fleeting moment just before the alarm goes off.

Witlag: the delay between the delivery and comprehension of a joke.

A man answers his phone and has the following conversation: "Yes, mother, I've had a hard day. Gladys has been really difficult. I know, I should be more firm, but it's hard. Well, you know how she is. I remember you warned me, you told me that I shouldn't marry her. Well, you were so right. You want to speak to her? Okay." He calls into the next room, "Gladys, your mother's on the phone."

I once saw an office mate plug his power strip back into itself and couldn't for the life of him figure out why his system would not turn on.

If it ain't broke, fix it 'til it is.

The traffic light on our corner of Main Street buzzes when it's safe to cross the street. I was crossing with a co-worker and she asked what the buzzer was for. I explained that it was a signal for blind people.
She was appalled.
 "What on earth are blind people doing, driving?"

Reality is just a crutch for those people who can't cope with drugs.   -Robin Williams

It's hard to understand how a cemetery raised its burial costs and blamed it on the cost of living.

As long as there are tests, there will be prayer in public schools.

I wish the buck stopped here. I could use a few.

There is one sure cure for insomnia. Get more sleep.

Behind every successful man is a surprised woman.

When women are depressed they either eat or go shopping. Men invade another country.

A man walked into the Chamber of Commerce of a small town. He said in a desperate tone:
"Is there a criminal attorney in this town?"
To which one man said,
"Yes, but we can't prove it yet!"

A Red Sox fan got a really bad seat in the upper upper bleachers. Looking with his binoculars, he noticed an empty seat right on the third base line.
Thinking to himself, "What a waste," he made his way down.
When he arrived there, he asked the man next to the empty seat, "Is this seat taken?"
The man said, "This was my wife's seat. She was a great Red Sox fan."
"I'm really sorry for your loss. But, I'm wondering why you didn't give her seat to a friend or relative."
The man replied:
 "They're all at the funeral."

A 45-year-old woman who's had a facelift doesn't look 25. If it works, she looks like a well-rested 35-year-old woman. If it doesn't work, she looks like a Hallowe'en costume.
-Fran Lebowitz

If losing your head is a beheading, is liposuction a behinding?
-Flash Rosenberg

Old lawyers don't die, they lose their appeal.

I tried to drown my thoughts, but they learned to swim.

Sleep: that fleeting moment just before the alarm goes off.

My grandmother's 90. She's dating. He's 93. It's going great. They never argue. They can't hear each other.

It's been so long since I made love, I can't even remember who gets tied up.
-Joan Rivers

Work is the price you pay for money.

It's not true that life is one damn thing after another. It's the same damn thing over and over.
> -Edna St. Vincent Millay

98% of the adults in this country are hard-working, decent, honest Americans. It's the other lousy 2% that get all the attention. But then, we elected them.
> -Lily Tomlin

If you have to ask the price, you can't afford it. But if you <u>can</u> afford it, tell everyone what you paid.

Before drawing boards were invented, what did they go back to?

Laugh now, but one day you'll be driving a big Cadillac, wearing white shoes and belt, and eating dinner at four o'clock in the afternoon.

Spring forward, Fall back, Winter in Miami.

Why are lawyers buried ten feet underground? Because deep down, they're really not that bad.

Ever stop to think and forget to start again?

The more people I meet, the more I like my dog.

A site foreman had ten very lazy men working for him. One day, he decided to trick them into working. "I've got a really easy job today," he announced. "Will the laziest guy here please put up his hand?" Nine hands went up. "How come you didn't put your hand up?" he asked the tenth man. "Too much trouble," came the reply.

My mother always said don't marry for money, divorce for money.

The Gettysburg Address is 269 words, the Declaration of Independence is 1,337 words, and the Holy Bible (not known which version) is 773,00 words.

The tax law in the United States, however, has grown from 11,400 words in 1913 to seven million words today. Taxes eat up 38.2% of a family's income.

I try to pay my taxes with a smile.
But they always insist on cash.

A couple was driving down a lovely country road, enjoying the scenery, when they drove into a deep muddy hole and could not get out. The road was not a familiar one and they didn't know what to do. As luck would have it, along came a farmer and his horse. The farmer offered to pull the car out of the hole for $50 and the relieved couple agreed. In ten minutes, they were free. "You know," the farmer said, "you're the tenth car I've pulled out of the mud today." The husband looked around and asked, "When do you have time to take care of your land? At night?"
"No," said the farmer. "That's when I put water in the hole."

An oboe is a Cockney tramp.

Staying married may have long-term benefits. You can elicit much more sympathy from friends over a bad marriage than you ever can from a good divorce.
-P.J. O'Rourke

Holy smoke: a church on fire.

I'm blonde. What's your excuse?

THINGS IMPOSSIBLE TO SAY WHEN DRUNK
1. Thanks, but I don't want to sleep with you.
2. Nope, no more drinking for me!
3. Sorry, but you're really not my type.
4. Good evening Officer, isn't it a lovely night tonight?
5. I'm not interested in fighting you.
6. Oh, I just couldn't ... nobody wants to hear me sing.
7. Thank you, but I wouldn't dare try to dance. I don't know how.
8. I must be going home now. I have work to do in the morning.

My wife told me we couldn't afford beer any more so I'd have to give it up. A day later, I saw her spending $100 on makeup. So I asked her how come I had to give up my stuff but she didn't.
She said she needed the makeup to look pretty to me.
I told her that's what the beer was for.
I don't think she's coming back.

My divorce came to me as a complete surprise. That's what happens when you haven't been home in eighteen years.
-Lee Trevino

In Hollywood, an equitable divorce settlement means each party getting fifty percent of the publicity.
                    -Lauren Bacall

A lot of people ask me how short I am. Since my last divorce, I think I'm about $100,000 short.
                    -Mickey Rooney

The judge had just awarded a divorce to Beth, who had requested support payments. He said to the now ex-husband, "I have decided to give your wife $400 a month for support."
"That's fine, Judge," said the ex.
"And once in a while, I'll chip in a few bucks myself."

80% of American men kiss their wife goodbye when they leave the house.
10% kiss the house goodbye when they leave their wife.

At a party, there are two kinds of people: those who want to stay until the end and those who want to leave early. The trouble? they're usually married to each other.

After being married for 30 years, a man said, "Honey, do you realize that, 30 years ago, I had a cheap apartment, a cheap car, slept on a pull-out bed and watched a 13" B&W television...but I got to sleep every night with a hot 21-year-old blonde. You've put on a bit of weight, sometimes your roots show and your body isn't what it used to be. It seems to me you're not holding up your end of things."
Now the wife, a reasonable woman, told him he could go out and find a hot 21-year-old blonde. She'd make sure that he'd once again have a cheap apartment, a cheap car and be sleeping on a sofa-bed.

Marriage is a 3-ring circus. Engagement ring, wedding ring, and suffering.

My husband and I just split up. I finally faced the fact that we're incompatible. I'm a Gemini and he's a horse's ass.

What do you call a man who has lost 95% of his intelligence?
Divorced.

It's easier to get older than to get wiser.

Any time things seem to be going better, you've overlooked something.

Any tool dropped while repairing a car will roll underneath to the exact center.

Any sufficiently advanced technology is indistinguishable from magic.

Any task worth doing was worth doing yesterday.

We don't have the time or money to do it right, but we'll find the time and money to do it over again.

You know it's a bad day when your blind date is your ex-wife.

If you saw your ex-wife and her lawyer drowning in a swimming pool, what would you do? Go to lunch or take in a movie?

What should you do if you see your ex-husband rolling around in pain on the ground?
Shoot him again.

"Today, one year after their divorce, Pamela and Tommy Lee announced they're getting back together. You know what that means? There's still hope for Ike and Tina Turner."
-Jay Leno

Old deans don't die, they lose their faculties.

Junk is something you've kept for years and throw away 3 weeks before you
need it.

Families are like fudge, mostly sweet with a few nuts.

Middle age is when you choose your cereal for the fiber and not for the toy.

Laughing helps. It's like jogging on the inside.

Forgive your enemies. It messes up their heads.

Timing has a lot to do with the outcome of a rain dance.

Support your local Rescue Squad. Get lost!

CATS

Cats do pretty much what they want.

They rarely listen to you.

They're totally unpredictable.

They whine when they're unhappy.

When you want to play,
they want to be left alone.

When you want to be alone,
they want to play.

They expect you to cater
to their every whim.

They're moody.

They leave hair everywhere.

They drive you crazy and
cost an arm and a a leg.

Conclusion: they're tiny little women in cheap fur coats.

A man is sitting at home alone when he hears a knock on the front door.
He opens the door to find two sheriff's deputies standing there.
He asks if there is a problem.
One of the deputies asks if he is married.
He says, "Yes, I am."
The deputy then asks to see a picture of his wife. He gets one and hands it over.
The deputy says, "I'm very sorry, sir; but it looks like your wife's been hit by a truck."
The man replies: "I know, but she has a great personality, is an excellent cook, and I love her."

Remember...Once you get over the hill, you'll begin to pick up speed.

If it weren't for stress, I wouldn't have any energy at all.

Opportunities always look bigger going than coming.

Middle age is when broadness of the mind and narrowness of the waist change places.

Learn from the mistakes of others. Trust me...you can't live long enough to make them all yourself.

Everyone is entitled to my opinion.

"You seem to have more than the average share of intelligence for a man of your background," sneered the lawyer at a witness on the stand.
"If I wasn't under oath," replied the witness, "I'd return the compliment."

Life's golden age is when the kids are too old to need baby sitters and too young to borrow the family car.

Eat a live toad first thing in the morning and nothing worse can happen to you all day.

The best way to keep kids at home is to make the home a pleasant atmosphere... and let the air out of their tires. –D. Parker

Q: I'm two months pregnant now. When will my baby move?
A: With any luck, right after college.

AGE BEFORE BEAUTY

STORY FROM A KANSAS STATE HIGHWAY PATROL OFFICER

I pulled an elderly lady over the other day for speeding on U.S 166 Eastbound at Mile Marker 73. I asked for her driver's license, registration and proof of insurance.

She took out the required information and handed it to me with the other papers, I was somewhat surprised to see that she had a conceal carry permit. I asked her if she had a weapon in her possession at this time.

She said she had a .45 automatic in her glove box. Something made me want to ask if she had any other firearms in the vehicle. Yes, she had a 9mm Glock in her center console.

"Is that it?" I asked.

Well, she did have one more, a .38 special in her purse.

I then asked her what she was so afraid of.

She looked me right in the eye and said: "NOT A DAMN THING!"

At my age, "getting any" means sleep.

I don't think about dying... it's the last thing I want to do.

The future isn't what it used to be.

The operator at St. Mary's Hospital heard a sweet tremulous voice: obviously an elderly woman. "Who can tell me how a patient is doing?" she asked.
"I'll be glad to help you," the operator said. "Just give me the name and room number of the patient."
The old lady said, "Norma Fine, Room 203."
"I'll check and get back to you." After a few minutes, the operator returned and said that Norma was doing well, her blood pressure was back to normal and her physician had scheduled her to be discharged the next day.
"Thank you!" said the old lady. "That's wonderful news. God bless you!"
The operator replied: "You're perfectly welcome. Is Norma your daughter?"
'No," said the old lady. I'm Norma Fine in Room 203 and nobody tells me shit."

EAT RIGHT AND EXERCISE. DIE ANYWAY.

Sometimes I laugh so hard, the tears run down my leg.

Old budgets never die; they're filibustered.

Old cashiers never die; they just check out.

Don't let aging get you down. It's too damn hard to get back up.

With age comes some new skills. For instance, I can laugh, cough, sneeze, and pee—all at the same time.

LIVE EACH DAY AS IF IT WERE YOUR LAST. One day you'll get it right.

At my age, Happy Hour is a nap.

Five-year-old to her grandmother: "My teacher says little girls can grow up to be anything they choose. Why did you choose to be an old lady?"

Old bankers never die; they just lose interest.

Old man carrying his elderly wife, on the steps:
"No, I'm not tired...just trying to remember why we were going upstairs."

My father lived to 100, he said because of carrots. He never touched them.

Two elderly guys, one 80 and one 87, were sitting on a park bench one morning. The 87-year-old had just finished jogging and wasn't even breathing hard. The younger man asked him how he managed to have so much energy at his age.
"I eat rye bread every day," he said. "Not only does it give energy, but you'll have great stamina with the ladies...if you know what I mean."
The man knew exactly what he meant and stopped at a bakery on his way home.
"Do you have rye bread?" he asked the saleslady.
She said, "We have a whole shelf of it. Would you like a loaf?"
"I want five loaves."
"My goodness, five loaves! By the time you get to the third loaf, it'll be hard."
He replied, "I can't believe everyone in the world knows about this but me!"

Old hackers never die; they just go to bits.

I drive way too fast to worry about cholesterol.

Eventually, you will reach a point where you stop lying about your age and start bragging about it.

A doctor told an audience in Florida about the evils of red meat, salt, and sugar. "Who can tell me what food causes the most suffering?" From a 75-year-old came the answer: "Wedding cake."

To save money, the government is starting to deport seniors instead of illegals. Older folks are easier to catch and won't remember how to get home.
I started to cry when I thought of you and then it dawned on me...
of course, I'll see you on the bus!

Old blondes never fade, they just dye away.

I don't know how I got over the hill without ever making it to the top.

The older someone is, the longer they had to walk to get to school.

If things improve with age, I'm approaching magnificent.

An elderly couple stayed together although they hated each other. They were constantly fighting and the old man would shout, "When I die, I'll dig my way up and out of the grave and come back to haunt you!"

All the neighbors feared this old man. Whenever something strange happened, they would put the blame on him. When he died at 88, the entire neighborhood was relieved. His wife had a closed casket at the funeral.

After the burial, she went straight to a local bar and began to celebrate. Her neighbors went to keep an eye on her. One asked, "Aren't you afraid that he may indeed be able to dig his way out of the grave and come back to haunt you?"

The old lady put down her drink, smiled, and said, "Let him dig. I had him buried upside down...and, knowing him, he'll never ask for directions!"

More money is being spent on breast implants and Viagra, than on Alzheimer's research. This means in 2040 there should be an older population with perky breasts and fine erections...but no idea what to do with them.

A woman holding a baby sat in the pediatrician's examination room. The doctor arrived, examined the baby, checked his weight, and finding him a bit thin, asked if he were breastfed or fed with a bottle.
"Breast fed," she said.
"Well, please strip to your waist," said the doctor.
He gave her breast a very professional and detailed examination, kneading, pressing, and rubbing.
Motioning for her to get dressed, he said, "No wonder this baby is underweight. You don't have any milk."
"I know," she said. "I'm his Grandma.
"But I'm glad I came."

I was taught to always respect my elders, but they're getting harder and harder to find.

A man in an Old Soldiers' Home said to another: "Remember when we were sure they put saltpeter into the water to take our minds off sex?" When his friend nodded, he added: "Well, I think it's starting to work."

I'm so old, I lost a buttonhole.

My friend Harold had to spend a week in the hospital and a nurse there made him crazy. She spoke to him as if he were a small child. It was "how are we today?" and "are we hungry?" Getting fed up, Harold took his breakfast apple juice off the tray and saved it. When he was given a urine bottle to fill, you know where the juice went! The nurse came to pick it up and said, "My, it seems we are a little cloudy today." Harold snatched the bottle and drank it down, saying "Maybe I'll filter it better this time." The nurse fainted; but Harold just smiled.

My neighbor was outside, when a car came crashing into his yard. He rushed to help the elderly driver. "That was a close call!" he said. "And you look quite on in years to still be driving!"
"Well, yes, I am," said the old man proudly. "I'll be 97 next month. The last time I saw the doctor, he asked if I still had a driver's license.
He asked to see it and then cut it into pieces, and threw them in the basket.
'You won't be needing this anymore!' he said. Isn't that wonderful? I'm so old I no longer need a license!"

The man was in his 70s and he had a young knockout wife. They were shopping in an upscale boutique when an old friend of the man spotted them.
Eyeing the curvaceous young thing as she bent to try on a pair of stilettos, the friend said, "How in hell did you land a wife so young and hot?"
The man smiled. "I told her I'm 95."

George Burns, preparing to give a speech. "I'm very pleased to be here. Let's face it, at my age I'm pleased to be <u>anywhere.</u>"

"Blessed are the young, for they shall inherit the National Debt."
-Herbert Hoover

The upside of being senile is you can hide your own Easter eggs.

Another good thing about being poor is that when you turn seventy, your children will not have you declared legally insane in order to gain control of your estate.
-Woody Allen

There must be more to life than having it all.

A lady was driving on the highway. She always checked her speedometer to make sure she was within the speed limit.
It was the same this day; nevertheless, there it was in her rearview mirror: a police car, all lights flashing and definitely after her. Oh, lord, what have I done now? She wondered. I haven't been drinking, I wasn't speeding, I have my seat belt buckled. What could this be about?
In any case, she pulled over and waited in trepidation as the cop got out of his car and came over to her side. She rolled down her window as he spoke to her. Then she shook her head and pointed to her ear to tell him she was deaf.
The policeman smiled a little and knowing sign language, signed to her: "I know. I'm here to tell you your horn is stuck."

Interviewer: What's your birthday?
Retired Person: November 16th.
Interviewer: What year?
Retired Person: Every year.

Except for an occasional heart attack, I feel as young as I ever did."
                                    -Robert Benchley

"At my age, flowers scare me."
                              -George Burns

Retirement at 65 is ridiculous. When I was 65, I still had pimples."
                              -George Burns

"I'm at the age where just putting my cigar in its holder is a thrill.
                              -George Burns

For dying, you always have time.
                              –old Yiddish saying

Old policemen never die; they just cop out.

3 letters change a boy into a man: A G E.

The only trouble with retirement … you never get a day off!

Starting tomorrow, whatever life throws at me, I'm going to duck so it hits someone else.

These days, half the stuff in my shopping cart says, "For Fast Relief."

THE SENILITY PRAYER: Grant me the senility to forget the people I never liked anyway, the good fortune to run into the ones I do, and the eyesight to tell the difference.

The friend of a fellow aged 78 who had just married a younger woman, said to him: "How is married life?"
"Marvelous," he said. "We make love nearly every night. Nearly, on Monday ... Nearly, on Tuesday ..."

An elderly fellow named Keith
Misplaced his old set of false teeth.
They'd been laid on a chair,
He forgot they were there,
Sat down...and got bit underneath.

Here's how to prevent sagging...eat until the wrinkles all fill out.

An elderly woman decided to prepare her will and told her lawyer she had two final requests. First, she wanted to be cremated; and second, she wanted her ashes scattered all over Wal-Mart. "Why Wal-Mart?"
"Then I'll be sure my daughters visit me twice a week."

Old owls never die; they don't give a hoot.

I decided to take an aerobics class for seniors. I bent and twisted, gyrated, jumped up and down and perspired for over an hour.
But by the time I got my tights on, the class was over.

I very quietly confided to my best friend that I was having an affair.
She turned to me and asked, "Who's catering it?"
And that, my friends, is the definition of OLD.

Just before the funeral services began, the undertaker came up to the very elderly widow and asked, "How old was your husband?"
"98," she replied. "Two years older than me."
"So, you're 96!"
Said she, "Hardly worth going home, is it?"

Reporters interviewing a 104-year-old woman asked her what was the best thing about being 104.
She responded: "No peer pressure."

Boy, my age is certainly catching up with me! I've had two bypass surgeries, a hip replacement and new knees. I fought off cancer and diabetes. I'm half blind and quickly losing my hearing. I take 10 different medications and I'm sure some of them are making me dizzy and constipated. I can't remember my age sometimes and have lost nearly all my friends.
But thank God, I still have my driver's license!

My memory's not as sharp as it used to be. Also, my memory's not as sharp as it was.

Support your medical examiner. Die strangely.

If you laugh a lot, when you get old, your wrinkles will all be in the right places.

There's nothing wrong with the younger generation that twenty years or so won't take care of.

Old farmers don't die; they just go to seed.

Old chemists don't die; they fail to react.

I've known that woman for over 30 years; and she looks just the same. Terrible.

Three deaf old ladies were taking a stroll. The first said, "Wow, it's windy today!" The second said, "No, it's Thursday." And number three said, "So am I. Let's go get a drink."

A tone-deaf old person named Bing
When somebody asked him to sing,
Replied, "It is odd
But I cannot tell God
Save the Weasel from God save the King."

The census taker knocked on Ms. Barker's door.
 She answered all his questions, but one. She would not divulge her age.
"But everyone tells their age to the census taker," he told her.
"Did Ms. Barbara Hill and Ms. Dorothy Hill tell you their ages?"
"Why, yes they did."
"I'm about the same age as them."
"Old as the Hills," wrote the census taker.

Marie and Miriam meet for the first time in 50 years. Marie tells Miriam about her children, her seven grandchildren, and all the family news.
"So tell me, Miriam, how about your kids?"
"I'm sorry to say we don't have children or grandchildren," says Miriam.
"No children or grandchildren? So tell me, what do you do for aggravation?"

Old soldiers never die. Young ones do.

The couple is in their 70s. The wife tells her husband that her doctor thinks she should have intercourse ten times a month.
"That's fine," says her husband. "Put me down for three."

Old burglars never die, they just steal away.

Old mechanics never die; they just retire.

Q: As people age, do they sleep more soundly?
A: Yes, but usually in the afternoon.

At my age, every morning is the dawning of a new error.

A lady calls the local newspaper to order an obituary. She proceeds to tell the reporter all about her husband Jake, his early days, his struggles, his successes, his philanthropies, the family, the children, the grandchildren and on and on.
The reporter interrupts: "Madam, we charge five dollars a word."
She says, "So just put in 'Jake died.'"
"Madam, we have a five word minimum."
She thought for several moments. "Okay, so put in 'Jake died, Mercedes for sale.'"

Middle age is when you know your way around but don't feel like going.

Kevin has a terrible accident at work and is rendered impotent. He and his wife go to a specialist, who listens carefully and then says he can cure Kevin with a surgery that will cost $15,000.
He suggests they go home and talk it over.
A few days later, Kevin calls the doctor.
The doctor says, "Did you and your wife completely talk this over?"
"Yes, we did and she decided on granite countertops."

Charlie, a new retiree-greeter at Wal-Mart, just couldn't seem to get to work on time. Every day he was five, ten, or 15 minutes late. But he was a good greeter, really tidy, clean-shaven, sharp-minded and a real help to customers.

One day, the boss called him into the office for a talk.

"Charlie, I have to tell you, I like your work ethic. You do a bang-up job when you finally get here; but you being late so often is quite bothersome."

"I realize that, boss, and I'm working on it."

"Well, good, you are a team player. That's what I like to hear."

"Yes, sir. I will try to do better."

The manager had a puzzled look on his face.

"I know you're retired from the Armed Forces," he said.

"What did they say to you there if you were late so often in the morning?"

Charlie looked down at the floor, smiling. He chuckled quietly, then said with a grin:

"They usually saluted and said,
'Good morning, Admiral.
"Can I get your coffee, sir?'"

An elderly man who had had a bit too much to drink is driving home from the city one night and, of course, his car is weaving a bit. So a cop pulls him over.
"It looks to me," says the cop, "like you've had a few too many to drink this evening."
"I may have," says the drunk with a smile.
"Did you know," says the cop, folding his arms across his chest, "that a few intersections back, your wife fell out of the car?"
"Oh, thank God," says the driver.
"For a while there, I was sure I'd gone deaf!"

Middle age is when you burn the midnight oil at about 9:00 p.m.

It's no longer a question of staying healthy. It's a question of finding a sickness you like.
                                    -Jackie Mason

Old skateboarders never die; they just lose their bearings.

The nurse insisted that the old man in the hospital room must get into a wheelchair. In the elevator, she asked him if his wife was waiting. "She's upstairs," he said. "Changing out of her hospital gown.

A woman in the supermarket is following a grandfather and his grandson. It's obvious that he really has his hands full with this child, screaming for candy in the candy aisle, cookies in the baked goods section, and for fruit or soda or whatever he happens to see.
Grandpa is working his way along, looking at his list, saying over and over in a soft, tight voice, "Easy, William, it won't be long, boy." The woman goes to him and says, "You have the patience of Job. William is very lucky to have you for a grandfather."
"Thanks," says the old gent, "but I'm William. The little brat's name is Teddy."

Old tanners don't die; they go into hiding.

An elderly man shuffled slowly into an ice cream parlor and pulled himself, slowly and painfully, onto a stool.
After catching his breath, he ordered a banana split.
The waitress kindly asked: "Crushed nuts?
"No," he replied. "Arthritis."

I guess I'm old. I'm smiling because I can't hear a word you say. I'm the first one to find the bathroom, wherever I go. I'm very good at telling stories...over and over and over again. Yes, I guess I'm old.

There was an old man from Nantucket
Who kept all his cash in a bucket.
His daughter named Nan
Ran away with a man.
And as for the bucket, Nantucket.

Sam hasn't seen his friend Allen for a month and is worried.
Suddenly, there's Allen on his usual park bench. What happened? Sam wants to know.
Well, Allen says, remember that cute little blonde waitress at the diner? She filed rape charges against me! Me, 77 years old! I was so pleased that I went to court and pled guilty.
The judge gave me 30 days for perjury.

Q: Where can women over the age of 60 find young, sexy men who are interested in them?
A: Look in the bookstore under Fiction.

Here's a great idea: Let's put the senior citizens in jail and the criminals in nursing homes. With this one move, we solve two problems.

Seniors would have access to showers and hobbies. They would receive unlimited free prescriptions, dental care, wheel chairs—whatever they needed.

Bedding would be washed twice a week, all meals and snacks would be brought to them and they would have constant video monitoring, in case of a fall or heart attack.

They would have family visits in a suite built for that purpose. They would have access to a library, gym, pool, and an outdoor exercise yard complete with gardens. Their guards would have a code of conduct to be strictly adhered to, with attorneys available at no charge.

As for the criminals, they would get cold food, be left alone and unsupervised and be allowed to shower only once a week. They would live in tiny rooms for which they'd have to pay a lot. And they'd have no hope of ever getting out.

Sounds like a good idea, right?

Oh, and in addition, the seniors would be in a safe gated community.

A young man asked a rich old man how he made his fortune. The old guy cleared his throat and said, "Well, son, it was 1932, the depth of the Great Depression. I was down to my last nickel.

"I invested that nickel in an apple. I spent hours polishing that apple until it looked so beautiful I was able to sell it for ten cents.

"The next morning, I invested those ten cents in two more apples. I spent hours polishing them and at the end of the day was able to sell them for twenty cents.

You get the idea. I followed this system for a month, at the end of which I had accumulated exactly $1.37.

"Then my wife's father died and left us $2,000,000."

Doctor: Well, I have good news and bad news...
Patient: What's the bad news?
Doctor: I'm afraid you have Alzheimer's Disease.
Patient: That's awful! What's the good news?
Doctor: You can go home and forget all about it.

PERSPECTIVES ON AGING

I've gotten to the age where I need my false teeth and hearing aids before I can ask where my glasses are.

Age only matters if you're cheese.

Forget organic. I need all the preservatives I can get.

My mind not only wanders, sometimes it leaves completely.

The golden years: when actions creak louder than words.

Age is an issue of mind over matter. If you don't mind...it doesn't matter. –Mark Twain

Old age and treachery will overcome youth and skill.

Age doesn't always bring wisdom; sometimes it comes alone.

He who laughs, lasts.

What's the best birth control for elderly seniors?
Nudity.

An accident really uncanny
Befell an unfortunate granny.
She sat down in a chair
While her false teeth were there,
And bit herself right in the fanny.

I'm very proud of this gold pocket watch. My grandfather, on his deathbed, sold me this watch.
-Woody Allen

Three elderly ladies were discussing the travails of getting old.
Sometimes I find myself in front of the refrigerator," said the first lady, "and I can't remember why I went there."
The second lady said, "Well, sometimes when I'm on the stairs, I find I don't know if I'm going up or coming down."
"Well, ladies, I'm glad I don't have your problems," said the third.
"Knock wood." She rapped on the table and then said,
"That must be the door. I'll get it."

You know you're getting old when you stoop to tie your shoelaces and wonder what else you could do while you're down there.
-George Burns

A man's only as old as the women he feels.
–Groucho Marx

People ask me what I'd most appreciate getting for my 87th birthday. I tell them, a paternity suit.
–George Burns

Old janitors don't die; they kick the bucket.

Old actors never die, they just drop a part.

Don't cry because it's over; smile because it happened.

I don't feel old. I don't feel anything until noon. Then it's time for my nap. –Bob Hope

When I was a boy, the Dead Sea was only sick.
-George Burns

And now a word from the Old Age Home: HELP!

I don't plan to grow old gracefully. I plan to have face-lifts until my ears meet.
> -Rita Rudner

The secret of longevity is to keep breathing.
> -Sophie Tucker

At my age, I do what Mark Twain did. I get the daily paper, look at the obituary page, and if I'm not there, I carry on as usual.
> -Patrick Moore

At the age of 70, there are 5 women to every man.
Isn't that an ironic time for men to be getting those odds?

Old cows don't die; but they lose their whey.

Born free ...taxed to death.

When you're young, you want to be master of your fate and captain of your soul.
When you are older, you'll be glad to be master of your weight and captain of the bowling team.

Here's a little secret for building up your arm and shoulder muscles. Be careful to do it gradually.
Begin by standing straight with a 5-pound potato sack in each hand. Extend your arms straight out from your sides and hold that for as long as you can.
Eventually, try to reach a full minute. After a few weeks, move up to 10-pound sacks, then 20 pounds, then 50, and then, the ultimate, 100-pound sacks.
Try to hold them with outstretched arms for a full minute.
When you feel confident at that level, start putting a couple of potatoes in each sack, but be careful not to overdo it.

Old is when getting lucky means finding your car in the parking lot.

Old is when clothes you buy now will never wear out.

"How old is your Granddad?"
"I don't know, but we've had him a long time."

Old is when you are cautioned to slow down by the doctor instead of the police.

A man came to my door, collecting for the Old Age Home. So I gave him my husband.

I was taught to respect my elders, but it's getting pretty hard to find any.

A doctor advised his elderly patient to move to the quiet countryside where he would have fresh air and be able to sleep through the night. After he settled in, he took a walk and met another elderly man. "I'm here for my health," he said. "Is this really a healthy environment?"
"It sure is. When I first arrived here I couldn't say one word. I had hardly any hair on my head and didn't have the strength to walk across a room."
"That's wonderful," said the newcomer. "How long have you been here?"
"I was born here."

Old teachers never die, but they lose class.

Instant Old Woman: Just add coffee.

An elderly couple is lying in bed one morning, waking up from a good night's sleep. He takes her hand and she says, "Don't touch me!" "Why not?"
"Because I'm dead!"
The husband said, "What are you talking about? Here we are, speaking to each other." "I'm definitely dead," she insisted. "You are not dead," he said. "What in the world makes you think so?"
"Because I woke up this morning and nothing hurts!"

Two psychologists meet at their 25th college reunion. One of them looks pretty much as he had when he was a student. The other doctor is withered and wrinkled.
The older-looking one asks, "What's your secret, Bob? Listening to other people's problems day after day, year after year has made an old man of me."
The other one says, "Who listens?"

It was a family funeral. The deceased was universally hated. Was there something good to say about him? Finally, someone got up and said, "His brother was worse."

An elderly lady finished her shopping at Wal-Mart and, upon returning to her car, found four males in it and the car was pulling out. She dropped all her shopping bags, pulled out a handgun and screamed at the top of her voice, "I have a gun and I know how to use it! Get out of the car, you little bastards!"

The young men didn't wait for an invitation, but exited the car and ran like crazy; whereupon the old lady, somewhat shaken, proceeded to load her shopping bags into the back of the car and got into the driver's seat. She found she just couldn't get her key to go into the ignition. Then it dawned on her why.

A few minutes later, she found her own car, the same make and color, parked four or five spaces away.

She loaded her car and drove to the police station. The desk sergeant nearly choked with laughter and pointed to the other end of the counter where four pale young men were reporting a car-jacking by a mad old woman described as white, small, with curly white hair, wearing glasses and carrying a Glock.

No charges were filed.

The 60-year-old woman had a miracle baby. Friends came to visit, in awe and wonder. One friend came over, wanting to see the baby but every time she asked the new mother, the subject was changed.
Finally, the new mother said, "You'll see him, you really will. I'm just waiting for him to cry."
"But why?" asked the friend.
"So I can find him."

A foundryman retired after 35 years. He seemed to be quite wealthy. He owned eight houses and quite a bit of land; yet he worked every working day for those 35 years. Nobody could figure out where he got his money.
His bosses knew that every day he pushed a wheelbarrow out, on his way home, with a little sand in it.
The guards probed and even emptied the barrow. Nothing. Nothing but sand.
On the day he retired, one of the guards said, "I know you were taking something out of here, something that you sold and made money on. But we can't figure it out. What was it? You can tell me now."
"Wheelbarrows."

The crusty old managing partner at the publishing house finally passed away, much to everyone's relief. But he still kept getting calls asking to speak with him. "I'm sorry, he's dead," his secretary told callers.
This happened over and over and she finally realized that it was the same voice every time. So the next time he called, she asked him why he kept calling. "I was one of the junior associates years ago; and I just like hearing you say it."

QUIZ FOR SENIORS
Q: How can you lift a zebra with one hand?
A: You'll never find a zebra with one hand.

Q: If it took 8 men 10 hours to build a wall, how long would it take 5 men to build it?
A: No time at all. The wall is already built.

Q: How can you drop an egg on a cement floor without breaking it?
A: Easy. Cement floors are hard to break.

Q: How can you increase the heart rate of an elderly husband.
A: tell him you're pregnant.

After an accident, an elderly woman stepped forward and prepared to help the victim.
She was asked to step aside by a man who announced:
"Everyone step back please!
I've had a course in first aid and I'm trained in CPR!"
The old woman watched what he did for a few minutes.
Then she tapped him on the shoulder.
"When you get to the part about calling a doctor," she said,
"I'm already here."

The elderly couple was having memory problems, so the doctor suggested they start writing everything down.
That evening, the wife asks for a bowl of ice cream. "Sure," he says. "Don't you think you should write that down?" "No, I can remember that." "Well," she says, "I like my ice cream with strawberries and whipped cream on top. Want to write that down?" "No, I can remember that."
He leaves and after about 15 minutes, returns, handing her a plate with bacon and eggs. She stares at the plate and then says angrily, "I told you to write it down! You forgot my toast!"

An 85-year-old goes for his annual physical. The doctor examines him but finds nothing obviously amiss. "You're getting on in years, Harry," says the doctor. "Have you noticed anything changing?"
"Well," says Harry, "I do think my eyesight is starting to fail a little; but it's compensating for that."
"What do you mean: compensating?"
"When I have to get up to go to the bathroom in the middle of the night, as soon as I open the bathroom door, the light goes on, and when I'm finished, it goes off as I leave."
The doctor is amazed at this and after Harry is gone, he calls his wife to tell her the story.
"Oh, no," she says, halfway between laughing and crying. "He's been peeing in the fridge again!"

An elegant, well-dressed, well-groomed elderly gentleman walked into an upscale cocktail lounge.
Seated at the bar was a lovely older woman. The gentleman seated himself next to her and said in a low and intimate tone,
"So tell me, do I come here often?"

The Levins and the Crawfords were new friends and were inviting each other for dinner at their homes. After one of these dinners, the women went into the kitchen and the two men were left to converse. Said Levin, "We went to dinner last week at a new restaurant. It was really good. I recommend it highly." Crawford said, "Sure, we'll give it a try. What's the name of the place?"

Levin thought and thought and finally he said, "You know that flower that you give on important occasions...the one that smells good but has thorns...?"

"You mean a rose?" said his friend.

"Yes, that's the one." He turned and yelled into the kitchen, "Rose, what's the name of that new restaurant we liked so much?"

An older man had suffered from hearing problems for a long time. Finally, he was fitted for hearing aids that allowed him, finally, to hear clearly. On his next checkup, the doctor said, "Your family must be so pleased that you can hear." Said the patient, "Oh, I haven't told them. I sit and listen to all the conversations. I've changed my will twice."

JIM: I still enjoy great sex at 67."
TIM: "Really?"
JIM: Which is handy, since I live at 65."

The 70 year old man thought his wife, Del, was losing her hearing; so he decided to test her. He quietly came in the front door and called, "Del, are you home?" No response. So he moved further into the house. "Del?" he called. "Are you here?" Still nothing. Finally, he reached the kitchen door and saw her, standing at the stove. "Now can you hear me?" he asked.
"Yes," said Del. "For the third time, YES."

Two elderly women. One says, "My husband passed last week. He went into the garden for a cabbage and just keeled over from a massive heart attack."
Said her friend. "What did you do?"
"What could I do? I opened a can of peas."

There was an old lady of Harrow
Whose morals were terribly narrow.
At the end of her paths
She had built two bird baths—
For the different sexes of sparrow.

This guy is 71, an avid fisherman. One afternoon, he's sitting in his boat when he hears a voice say, "Pick me up!" He thinks he must have imagined it, when he hears it again, clearly: "Pick me up!" He looks over the side of the boat and there, sitting on a lily pad, is a frog. "Didn't you hear me?" says the frog. "I told you to pick me up. Pick me up and kiss me and I'll turn into a gorgeous young woman who will want to marry you and make love to you day and night." The man stares at the frog for a minute or two, then leans over, picks it up and puts it in the big breast pocket of his fishing jacket. The frog yells, "Are you nuts? Did you hear what I told you? Kiss me and I become a beautiful—"The man interrupts the frog. "Yeah, I heard you. But at my age, I'd rather have a talking frog."

These days, I spend a lot of time thinking about the hereafter.
 I go to get something and then wonder what I'm here after.

Losing a husband can be hard. In my case, it was almost impossible.

"Bartender, I'll have another scotch with just two drops of water," said the elderly lady.
It was her fourth, and yet she seemed sober. The barman said, "I'm curious...why only two drops of water?"
"At my age," she said, "I'm at the point where I can hold my scotch. Water? That's another thing altogether."

Two very elderly ladies were enjoying the sunshine on a park bench in Miami. They had been meeting at the park every day for over 12 years, chatting and laughing.
One day, the younger of the two ladies said, "Please don't be angry with me, dear, but I'm so embarrassed. After all these years and all the things we've told each other ... What is your name? I'm trying and trying to remember, but it just won't come to me."
The older woman stared at her, looking very distressed and said nothing for two full minutes.
Finally, with tears in her eyes, she said, "How soon do you have to know?"

Walt Disney didn't die; he's just in suspended animation.

A school principal retired and bought a modest home which happened to be close to a Middle School. He moved in during the Summer and all was peace and quiet.

Then came the new school year and after school every day a group of boys came charging down the street, banging every trash can along the way.

After several weeks, the man went out front and said to boys, "I remember banging on garbage cans when I was your age. If you come by every day and bang, I will give you each a dollar."

The kids were elated and enthusiastic. After a few days, the old-timer stopped them again and said, "I'm afraid that I'll only be able to pay you fifty cents." They accepted his offer, although with a bit of grumbling.

A few days later, he met them again and said, "My Social Security check is late. I can only give you twenty-five cents. Is that okay?"

"A lousy quarter?" said their ringleader. "If you think we're going to beat on these cans for just twenty-five cents, you're nuts! No way, mister! We quit!"

And, once again, there was peace and quiet.

Yesterday I was at my local market, buying a large bag of Purina dog chow for my dog Jake, and was in the checkout line when a woman behind me asked if I had a dog. What did she think, I had an elephant?

So, because I am retired and have little to do, on impulse I told her that I didn't have a dog, I was starting the Purina Diet again; and added that I probably shouldn't, because the last time I tried it, I ended up in the hospital in Intensive Care.

But I had already lost 50 pounds because the Purina Diet was perfect. You load your pockets with the nuggets and every time you feel hungry you eat one or two. The food is nutritionally complete and I was going to try it again. (By this time, the line behind me was listening, enthralled.)

Horrified, she asked if I ended up in Intensive Care because the food was stale or poisonous in some way. I told her, No, I stopped to pee on a fire hydrant and a car hit me. I am not allowed to shop at that market any more.

Better watch what you ask retired people. They have time to think of crazy things to say.

When the priest slid open the panel in the confessional, the elderly woman on the other side said, "Father, during World War II a handsome young German knocked on my door and begged me to save him. I hid him in my attic." The priest said, "That was foolhardy. But there is no need to confess.""Oh, it's worse than that, Father. He began to repay me with sexual favors." The priest said, "Those were terrible times and you were young. It is not surprising, what you did. But that was a long time ago. You are indeed forgiven."
"Thank you, Father," she said. "That's a great load off my mind. But I have another question." The priest said, "What is that?" "Should I tell him the war is over?"

A young braggart working at a construction site made fun of one of the older workers. Finally, the older man was fed up. "I'll bet you a week's wages," he said, "that I can haul something in a wheelbarrow over to the next site that you can't haul back." "You're on, old timer!" The old man grabbed the wheelbarrow's handles and said, "Okay, dumb ass, get in!"

The Ultimate Bathroom Joke Book

PUNS AND GAMES

The Ultimate Bathroom Joke Book

He got a job at the bakery because he kneaded dough.

Velcro! What a rip-off!

My brother used to be a banker; but then he lost interest.

Venison for dinner again? Oh deer!

Be kind to your dentist. He has fillings, too.

When you get a bladder infection, urine trouble.

I didn't like my beard at first. But then it grew on me.

She dropped out of Communism class because of bad Marx.

Protons have mass? I didn't even know they were Catholic.

They told me I was gullible and I believed them.

PMS jokes are not funny. Period.

Shotgun wedding: a case of wife or death.

If swimming keeps you slim, explain whales.

England has no kidney bank, but it does have a Liverpool.

I know a guy who's addicted to brake fluid. He says he can stop any time.

I changed my iPod's name to Titanic. It's syncing now.

I'm reading a book about anti-gravity. I can't put it down.

What do you call a dinosaur with an extensive vocabulary?
A thesaurus.

This girl said she recognized me from the vegetarian club, but I never met herbivore.

I wrote a theatrical performance about puns. It's a play on words.

They told me I have type A blood but it was a typO.

Did you hear? The cross-eyed teacher lost her job because she couldn't control her pupils.

All the toilets in the New York Police Department have been stolen. The cops have nothing to go on.

Why were the Indians here first? They had reservations.

    A Scots painter named Mack often thinned his paint to make it go a wee bit further.
Nobody knew this and one day the local church hired him to repaint their church.
Yes, he thinned down the paint and got the job because of his low bid.
    He was nearly finished when there was a clap of thunder followed by a hard rain and all the paint washed away.
    Mack cried to heaven: "Oh God, oh God, forgive me and tell me what to do!"
And a mighty voice thundered:
    "Repaint!   Repaint! And thin no more!"

I'd call him a sadistic, hippophilic necrophile, but that would be beating a dead horse.

MY INCONCLUSIVE TRAVEL PLANS FOR THIS YEAR

I've never been in Cahoots but apparently you can't go alone.
I've also never been in Cognito. I hear nobody recognizes you there.
I have, however, been in Sane, briefly. They have no airport; you must be driven there.
I'd love to visit Conclusions but you have to jump, and I'm not much on physical activity these days.
I've also been in Doubt but it's a sad place and I try not to go there.
Sometimes I'm in Capable and I go there more often than I used to.
One of my favorite places to be is in Suspense. It's an exciting place, and gets the heart pumping.
I have been in Flexible but I greatly regret going there.
And I think I may have been in Continent but I don't remember where it was.
It's an age thing.

Glibido: all talk and no action.

He took a ruler to bed to see how long he slept.

The cartoonist was found dead in his home. Details are sketchy.

A man rushed into a busy doctor's office and shouted, "Doctor, help me, I'm shrinking!" The doctor replied, "Take it easy. You'll just have to be a little patient."

A marine biologist developed a race of genetically engineered dolphins that could live forever if they were fed a steady diet of seagulls. One day, his supply of the birds ran out so he had to go out and trap some. After he had enough, he started back. On his way, he spied two lions asleep on the road. Afraid to wake them, he gingerly stepped over them.
Immediately, he was arrested and charged with transporting gulls across sedate lions for immortal purposes.

Evidence has been found that William Tell and his family were avid bowlers. Unfortunately, all the Swiss league records were destroyed in a fire and so we will never know for whom the Tells bowled.

A skeptical anthropologist was cataloging South American folk remedies with the assistance of a tribal brujo who indicated that the leaves of a particular fern were a sure cure for any case of constipation. When the anthropologist expressed his doubts, the brujo looked him in the eye and said sternly;
"Let me tell you—with fronds like these, you don't need enemas."

I stayed up all night to see where the sun went. Then it dawned on me.

She put lipstick on her forehead to help her make up her mind.

Two chefs in Boston were competing for the title of Finest Fish Fryer. Their talents were equal, their dishes equally excellent. Then, at the last moment, one of the chefs glazed his entry and won the title. "Alas," cried the loser. "There but for the glaze of cod go I!"

If you step into a plane and see your neighbor Jack sitting there, please don't yell, "Hi, Jack!"

A stevedore was in charge of offloading wheat from the ships at the harbor. Unfortunately, the wheat was quite moist and was not being sucked up easily by the vacuum. He approached the foreman for some advice, and was told: "If at first you don't suck seed, try drier grain."

TAKE THIS QUICK IQ TEST!
Don't cheat because then the test would be no fun.
There are no tricks to this test. I promise.
Just read this sentence:
FINISHED FILES ARE THE RESULT OF YEARS OF SCIENTIFIC STUDY COMBINED WITH THE EXPERIENCE OF YEARS.
Now count the f's in the sentence. Just once, please.
- How many did you count?
- A person of average intelligence finds three.
- If you spotted four, you're above average.
- If you got five...that's excellent!

But there are six of them. No catch. Many people read right over the word "of" without recording the 'f', because it sounds like a 'v.' Pretty weird, right?

DIVORCE: future tense of marriage.

The maker doesn't want it, the buyer doesn't use it, and the user doesn't see it. What is it?
Don't peek.
....A coffin

In what year did Christmas and New Year's fall in the same year?
They are always in the same year, New Year's in the beginning and Christmas at the end.

Which is correct to say: The yolk of the egg are white or The yolk of the egg is white?
Well...neither. The yolk is yellow.

Before Mount Everest was discovered, what was the highest mountain on earth?
Mt. Everest, silly. It was always there, but hadn't yet been named.

He drove his expensive car into a tree and found out how the Mercedes bends.

Taytr: a lecherous Mr. Potato Head.

A child is born in Boston, Massachusetts to parents who were both from Boston, Massachusetts, yet this child is not a United States citizen. How can this be?
She was born before Massachusetts was admitted to the Union, on February 6, 1788.

A man bragged that his grandfather had received a sword from his battalion, engraved with these words: "To Captain Jones, for bravery, daring and leadership during World War I. From the men of Battalion 8."
His friend said, "That story is obviously false." And it was. Why?
Our first war in Europe was known as the Great War. It was called World War I only after World War II had begun.

To some, marriage is a word; to others, a sentence.

It was an emotional wedding. Even the cake was in tiers.

I prefer to remain anomalous.

My bank says "24 hour banking" but I really don't have that much time. –S. Wright

I know a blonde who called me to get my number.

That same girl studied for a blood test.

And she sent me a fax with a stamp on it.

While hiking in the woods, Nate and Tom found this huge rock which had an old iron lever attached to it.
 Etched into the rock was this warning: "If the lever is pulled, the world will come to an end."
Nate was not superstitious and he wanted to pull the lever; but Tom was a bit paranoid and greatly feared that the sign was right.
He told Nate that if he tried to pull the lever, he'd shoot him!
Nate didn't believe his old friend would do such a thing so he lunged for the lever.
Sure enough, Tom shot him!
What is the moral of this story?
Better Nate than lever.

There are two types of people: those who divide people into two types of people, and those who do not.

How young can you die of old age?

Two brooms were hanging in the closet and after a while they got to know each other so well, they decided to get married.
One broom, of course, was the bride broom and the other, the groom broom.
After the wedding, at the wedding dinner, the bride broom leaned over and said to the groom broom, "I think I am going to have a little whisk broom."
"Impossible!" cried the groom broom. "We haven't even swept together!"

My friend missed the 44 bus, so she took the 22, twice.

On a very windy day, my friend and I were inside a park building, looking out at a very tiny lady, the area's custodian, whose job was to clear away leaves and debris left by visitors. She was working very hard, but the wind kept messing up her work. At times it looked as if she'd be blown away herself. We went out and said, "You're having a hard time in this wind. Why don't you put rocks in your shoes?"
To which she said, "You mean, now I weigh me down to sweep?"

A scientist finally succeeded in cloning himself but all his clone could do was sit and spew out curse words.
After a week of this, the scientist finally got fed up and pushed his clone out of his 10th-floor office building.
Not long after, there was a knock on his door. The scientist opened the door to see a policeman, who said, "I'm going to have to arrest you for making an obscene clone fall."

I believe that we should all pay our tax bills with a smile.
I tried that, but they wanted cash.

I know someone so stupid he thought Meow Mix was a cd for cats.

A young man in my town was infatuated with a young woman at his office, but he was so timid that he never could raise the courage to even speak to her. He told his therapist that when he came near her, he felt like nothing more than a tiny pebble. "Well," said the therapist. "If you want to get that girl you'll just have to be a little boulder."

Every night after work, Joe would get a six pack, bring it home and drink beer while he watched sports on tv. One night as he finished his last beer, the doorbell rang. He opened the door to a giant cockroach who punched him in the stomach and left. The next night, when he answered to door, that same cockroach grabbed him by the collar and threw him across the room, and then left. By the third night, Joe had given up drinking at all; but when he answered the door, there was that same cockroach who punched him around the face, and left.
The following day, Joe decided he needed medical attention. He went to see his doctor and told him what had been going on. "Can you help me?" he asked.
"No, sorry," said the doctor, "I can't do much. There's just a nasty bug going around."

I know a guy who spent twenty minutes just looking and staring at the orange juice can. Can you guess why?
Because it said CONCENTRATE.

My friend thinks a quarterback is a refund.

What is one thing all people, regardless of religion or politics, agree is between heaven and earth?
The word 'and.'

How can you rearrange the letters in the words 'new door' to make one word?
There's only one right answer.
Answer: 'one word.'

How many times can you subtract the number 5 from the number 25?
Only once; after that, it becomes 20.

A woman married ten different men in New Haven, yet she didn't break any laws. None of the men died and she never divorced. How can this be?
She was a Justice of the Peace.

The Canary Islands in the South Pacific are named after what animal?
The dog. In Latin, Insularia Canaria

When do Russians celebrate the October Revolution? November. Their calendar is 13 days behind ours.

A VERY LONG POTATO STORY

You know that all potatoes have eyes. Well, Mr. And Mrs. Potato had eyes for each other and got married and had a little sweet potato, who they named Yam.
Of course, they wanted the best for Yam. When it was time, they warned her about going out and getting half-baked, so she wouldn't accidentally get smashed and get a name for herself like "Hot Potato" and end up with a bunch of Tater Tots.
Yam said not to worry, no Spud would get her into the sack and make a rotten potato out of her! But on the other hand she wouldn't stay home and become a couch potato, either. She wanted to travel.
When she went off to Europe, her parents told Yam to watch out for the hard-boiled guys from Ireland, and those skinny guys called French Fries. And when she came back and took a trip out West, she was warned to watch out for Indians so she wouldn't get scalloped. Yam promised to stay good; she wouldn't associate with those snobs, the Yukon Golds; or the ones from the other side of the tracks who advertise their trade on trucks saying Frito Lay.

Finally, she settled down and went to Idaho P.U. (Potato University) hoping that after she graduated, she'd be in the chips. But in spite of all her parents did for her, one day Yam came home and said she was going to marry Scott Pelley. Her parents were very upset at this news and told Yam she could never marry Scott Pelley because ...
are you ready for this?
...because he was just a Common Tator.

Connie Cutler was born on December 27th, yet her birthday is in the summer. How can this be?
She lives in the Southern Hemisphere.

Even if they are starving, natives of the Arctic will never eat the eggs of a penguin. Why not?
Penguins live in the Antarctic.

What color is a purple finch?
Definitely red.

Dyslexics of the world...untie!

Pictures of missing husbands should be put on beer cans.

A scientist finds evidence of actual dinosaurs living in the rain forests of South America. He finally gets a grant to launch an expedition and away they go, a dozen or so scientists, plus attendants and guides, traveling by motor launch up the Amazon River.
After several weeks of finding nothing, the expedition party stumbles upon a three-foot-tall pygmy examining a 60-foot-long and very much dead spinosaurus.
The head scientist approaches the pygmy and says, "Did you kill this animal?"
"Yes," says the pygmy. "I did."
"But it's so very big and you're...excuse me...but you are quite small."
"Both things are true," says the pygmy.
"How on earth did you manage to kill it?"
"With my club."
All the scientists exchange disbelieving looks.
How on earth could this little person manage to kill such an extremely large animal with such a weapon?
"With your club? How big is your club?"
The pygmy replied:
"Well, there are about a hundred of us."

Why are 1990 American dollar bills worth more than 1989 American dollar bills?
1,990 dollar bills are one more than 1,989.

In Carlsbad, New Mexico, you cannot take a picture of a man with a wooden leg.
Why not?
Because the only way to take pictures is with a camera.

What animal gives us catgut?
Sheep and horses.

What is black when you buy it, red when you use it, and gray when you get rid of it?
Charcoal, of course.

When asked this riddle, 80% of kindergarten students got the answer, compared with 17% of Stanford U. seniors.

> What is greater than God
> More evil than the devil
> The poor have it.
> The rich need it.
> What is it?

Give up? The answer is...nothing.

This is like an optical illusion, with numbers. This riddle MUST be done in your head. You MAY NOT use pencil and paper. Try it...it's pretty strange.
- Take 1000 and add 40 to it.
- Now add another 1000.
- Now add another 30.
- Now add another 1000.
- Now add 20.
- Now add another 1000.
- Now add 10.
- What is the total?

Did you get 5,000? Seems most people do. But the real answer is:
4100.
Don't believe it? Use the calculator and see for yourself.

Did you hear about the restaurant on the moon? Great food, no atmosphere.

A murderer is condemned to death. He is to choose between three rooms: one is full of fire; the second, with poisonous snakes; and the third, filled with lions who haven't eaten for three years. Which is safest?
Why, the room with the lions. If they haven't eaten in three years...they're dead.

You have two plastic jugs filled with water. How could you put both into a barrel without any divider and be able to tell which water came from which jug?
Freeze 'em. Then put them into the barrel. After they thaw, you'll know which water came from where.

Can you name three consecutive days without using the words Sunday, Monday, Tuesday, Wednesday, Thursday, Friday, or Saturday?
Sure you can. Yesterday, Today, Tomorrow.

Why are soldiers so tired on April 1st?
Because they just had a 31-day March.

I'm apathetic and I don't care.

A woman shoots her husband, holds him underwater for over five minutes, then hangs him. Yet 5 minutes later, they go out together. How can this be so?
She is a photographer. She shot a picture, put it in developer, then hung it up to dry.

What award did they give the man who invented the door knocker?
The no-bell prize.

This is a most unusual paragraph.
I'm curious how quickly you can find out what is so unusual about it.
It looks so plain, you would think nothing was wrong with it. In fact, nothing IS wrong with it! It is just unusual, that's all.
Study it, think about it, work at it and you may find out what is odd. Try to do it without any coaching, if you don't mind.
Give up? Here's the answer. The letter 'e' which is the most common letter in the English language, does not appear even once in the entire paragraph.

Those who jump off a bridge in Paris are in Seine.

Once I got angry at the chef of an Italian restaurant and I gave him a pizza my mind.

No matter how much you push the envelope, it'll still be stationery.

Marathon runners with bad footwear know the agony of de feet.

Two silkworms had a race and ended up in a tie.

A man, carrying a limp and obviously very ill dog, runs into a veterinarian's office, yelling for help. The vet puts the dog on his examining table and, after a few minutes of examination, tells the man that his dog is dead. The man won't accept this. He asks for a second opinion.

The vet goes into the back and comes back with a cat which he places next to the dog's body. The cat walks up and down, next to the inert body, sniffing and poking with a paw and finally looks at the vet and meows. "I' m sorry," says the vet, "But the cat thinks your dog is dead, too."

The man is still unwilling to accept that his pet has died. The vet goes into the back with the cat and comes back with a black Labrador retriever.

The dog sniffs the body, walking back and forth, head to tail; and finally looks up and barks. "I'm sorry," says the vet, "but my dog says your dog is gone."

Finally resigned, the man asks how much he owes. $650," says the doctor.

"$650—just to tell me my dog is dead?"

"Well," the vet replies. "It's $50 for my first diagnosis. "The rest is for the cat scan and lab report."

Remember Buckwheat of Our Gang? Well, he has converted to Islam and changed his name to Kareem of Wheat. (I do hope he doesn't become a cereal killer.)

Most people don't know that the famous ship, Titanic, was carrying 12,000 jars of Hellman's mayonnaise which, in 1912, was manufactured in England. These jars were intended for delivery in Vera Cruz, Mexico which was to be the next port after New York City.
The Mexican people were eager awaiting delivery of these jars and were very sad at the terrible loss. So disconsolate were they that they declared a national day of mourning. It is known, of course, as….
Sinko de Mayo.

Humpty Dumpty, the tooth fairy, an old drunk and an honest attorney are all walking down the street together. Simultaneously, they each spot a $100 bill. Who finally gets that bill?
The old drunk, of course. The others are fairy tale figures.

A Russian couple was walking down the street in Moscow one evening, when the man felt a cold drop on his nose.
"I think it's raining," he said to his wife.
"Felt more like snow to me, Igor," she said.
"No, no, Sonya, I'm sure it was rain."
Well, they were well on the way to a major argument about whether it was raining or snowing when they spotted a minor official walking toward them.
"Let's not fight about it," said Igor. "We'll ask Comrade Rudolph. He'll know the official weather report."
When the official was nearby, Igor called out, "Comrade, can you tell us whether it is officially snowing or officially raining?"
"It is raining, of course," said the comrade.
"It certainly felt like snow to me!" Sonya insisted.
Igor quietly replied: "Rudolph the Red knows rain, dear."

The boss calls Ed into his office and asks him if he believes in life after death. Ed is very surprised at the question and says, "Of course not. There's no proof of it." His boss says, "Well, there is now. After you left early yesterday for your brother's funeral, he came here looking for you."

There was a haunted house on the outskirts of town which was avoided by everyone. But an enterprising young newspaper photographer decided it would make a terrific story if there really were a ghost living in the house and he, with his trusty camera, could take a few shots of the thing. Sure enough, when he entered the house in the wee hours of the morning, the ghost made an appearance, hoo-hoo'ing and clanking his chains.
"I mean you no harm," said the young man. "I just want to take your picture." The ghost was very happy to oblige and make headlines that would be positive for a change. He (or she) posed for a number of shots, upstairs and in the cobwebbed attic and in the gloomy basement. The happy photographer raced back to his darkroom and began developing his photos.
Sadly, they turned out to be underexposed and were totally black.
What message do we get from this story? The spirit was willing but the flash
was weak.

Why didn't the melons get married?
Because they cantaloupe.

The Lone Ranger and Tonto walked into a bar one day and sat down to have a beer. After a few minutes, a big tall cowboy walked in and said, "Who owns the big white horse tied outside?"

The Lone Ranger stood up, hitched his gunbelt, and said, "I do. Why?"

The cowboy said, "I just thought you would like to know that your horse is just about dead outside."

The Lone Ranger and Tonto rushed outside and, sure enough, Silver was almost dead from heat exhaustion. They got him water and soon the animal was feeling better.

The Lone Ranger said to Tonto, "I want you to run around Silver and see if you can create enough of a breeze to help him in this heat."

Tonto said, "Okay, Kemosabe," and took off, running circles around the horse. Satisfied that enough was being done, the Lone Ranger went back into the bar. Another cowboy came in and asked, "Who owns that big white horse outside?"

The Lone Ranger said, "I do. Why? What's wrong with him now?"

"I just wanted you to know you left your injun running."

What did the traffic light say to the car?
Don't look, I'm changing.

Why did the boy throw the clock out the window?
Because he wanted to see time fly!

How do you repair a broken tomato?
Tomato paste.

What did the hamburger name his daughter?
Patty.

How did the farmer mend his pants?
With cabbage patches.

Two robins were basking in the sun. Two really hungry cats spotted them.
"What's to eat?" said one cat.
Spotting the birds nearby, the second cat said, "How about some Baskin' Robbins?"

How much does a pirate pay for corn?
A buccaneer!

What's the difference between God and a lawyer?
God doesn't think he's a lawyer.

An Indian chief was feeling very sick, so he called for the medicine man.
After a brief examination, the shaman took out a long thin strip of elk hide from his medicine bag and told the chief to bite off, chew, and swallow one mouthful every day. "Should last you about half a moon," he said. Two weeks later, the medicine man came back to check on the chief. "How you feeling, chief?" he asked.
The chief shrugged. "The thong is gone," he said sadly, "but the malady lingers on."

A great Assyrian king was running low on treasure.
He decided to pawn his greatest treasure, known as the Star Diamond.
The pawnbroker offered him 100,000 dinar. The king protested: "But I paid a million for it! And how can you be so cheap with your king?" The pawnbroker replied:
 "When you wish to pawn a Star, makes no difference who you are."

What do you call a toothless bear?
A gummy bear.

Forget world peace. Try to visualize using your turn signal.

WIT AND WISDOM

SUCCESS
At age 4, success is not peeing in your pants.
At age 12, success is having friends.
At age 17, success is having a driver's license.
At age 21, success is getting laid.
At age 35, success is having money.
At age 50, success is having money.
At age 60, success is getting laid.
At age 70, success is having a driver's license.
At age 75, success is having friends.
At age 80, success is not peeing in your pants.

A woman settled down in her seat as the train left Grand Central for New Haven. The guy next to her pulled out his cellphone and proceeded with a very loud conversation: "Yes, sweetheart, it's Eric...I know it's a later train but I had a meeting...no, not with the redhead from accounts...you're the only one..." and on and on. When the train pulled into Larchmont, his seatmate yelled at the top of her voice, "Eric, turn the phone off and come to bed!" Wanna bet Eric doesn't use his cell in public anymore?

After every air cargo flight, the pilots fill out a form called a gripe sheet and the mechanics write their solutions on the same sheet. Here are some real-life complaints and their solutions.

Pilot: Left inside main tire almost needs replacing.
Ground
Crew: Almost replaced left inside main tire.
P: Test flight OK except auto-land very rough.
GC: Auto-land not installed on this aircraft.
P: Something loose in cockpit.
GC: Something tightened in cockpit.
P: Dead bugs on windshield.
GC: Live bugs on back-order.
P: Autopilot in altitude-hold produces a 200-foot-per-minute descent.
GC: Cannot reproduce problem on ground.
P: DME volume unbelievably loud.
GC: DME volume set to more believable level.
P: Number 3 engine missing.
GC: Engine found on right wing.
P: Aircraft handles funny.
GC: Aircraft warned to straighten up and be serious.

They keep telling us we have to get in touch with our bodies. Mine isn't all that communicative; but I heard from it Tuesday morning when I genially proposed,
 "Body, how'd you like to go to the 9 o'clock class in advanced toning and resistance?" Clear as a bell, my body said, "Listen, kiddo, do it and you die!"
-Molly Ivins

A recent study found that the average American walks about 900 miles a year. Another study found that on average, Americans drink 22 gallons of alcohol each year. This means that the average citizen gets about 41 miles to the gallon. Makes you damned proud to be an American!

Anything not nailed down is a cat toy.

Skinny people piss me off! Especially when they say things like, "Sometimes I forget to eat." Now, I might forget my address, my mother's maiden name, my keys, and my wallet. But I've never forgotten to eat. You have to be a special kind of stupid to forget to eat.
And screw you! In that case, you don't deserve to eat!   -Marsha Warfield

If a married Jewish man is walking alone in a park and expresses an opinion without anybody hearing him...is he still wrong?

A distraught Senior Citizen phoned her doctor's office. "Is it true," she asked, "that the new medication you prescribed must be taken for the rest of my life?" "I'm afraid so," said the doctor. After a moment's silence, she said, "I'm wondering, then, just how sick I am. Because this prescription says NO REFILLS."

A driver was stuck in bad traffic in Washington, DC. Nothing was moving.
A man knocked on his window and he rolled it down.
"What's going on?"
"Terrorists are holding Congress hostage in their building, asking for a $199 million dollar ransom. Otherwise, they are going to douse all of them in gasoline and set them on fire.
"We're going from car to car, collecting donations."
"How much is everyone giving, on average?" asked the driver.
"Roughly a gallon," was the answer.

The Ultimate Bathroom Joke Book

THE LATE GREAT BOB HOPE

ON TURNING 70: I still chase women, but only downhill.

ON TURNING 80: That's the time of your life when your birthday suit needs pressing.

ON NEVER WINNING AN OSCAR: Welcome to the Academy Awards or, as we call it, Passover.

ON GOLF: Golf is my profession. Show business is just to pay the greens fees.

ON BANKING: A bank will lend you money if you can prove you don't need it.

ON RECEIVING THE CONGRESSIONAL GOLD MEDAL: I feel very humble, but I think I have the strength of character to fight it.

ON HIS EARLY POVERTY: We all slept in the one bed. When it got cold, Mother threw on another brother.

ON HIS 6 BROTHERS: I learned to dance waiting for the bathroom.

A modern Orthodox Jewish couple, preparing for their wedding, meet with their Rabbi. He asks if they have any questions before the big day.

The man says, "We realize it's tradition for men to dance with men and women with women; but we'd like to dance together."

"Absolutely not," says the rabbi. "It's immodest. Men and women MUST dance separately.

"What about sex?"

"Of course! Sex with your wife to have children is a mitzvah!"

"What about different positions?"

"No problem. It's a mitzvah!"

"Woman on top? Doggy style? On the kitchen table?"

"Yes, certainly. Anywhere. It's a mitzvah!"

"Can we do it on rubber sheets with a bottle of hot oil, a couple of vibrators, a leather harness, a pot of honey, and a porno video?"

"You may indeed."

"Can we do it standing up?"

"No, you cannot," says the rabbi.

"But...why not?"

"Could lead to dancing!"

FROM THE MINDS OF WOMEN

Someday, when you have your own kids, you will understand why Mommy drinks.

Women are not moody. We simply have days when we are not inclined to put up with your bullshit.

I am fluent in three languages...English, sarcasm, and profanity!

Oh, how nice. Let me just jot that down on my list of what I don't give a crap about.

When a woman says, "What?" it's not because she didn't hear you. She's giving you a chance to change what you said.

When you really want to slap someone, do it and say, "Mosquito!"

The speed with which a woman says, "nothing" when asked what's wrong, is inversely proportional to the severity of the fight that's coming.

I never repeat gossip, so listen carefully.

PAULA POUNDSTONE, VERY WITTY & WISE

The wages of sin are death; but by the time taxes get taken out, it's just sort of a tired feeling.

The problem with cats is that they get the exact same look on their face whether they see a moth or an ax-murderer.

I don't have any money and I can't have a bank account because I don't know my mother's maiden name.

My mother said she learned how to swim when someone took her out in the lake and threw her off the boat.
I said, "Mom, they weren't trying to teach you how to swim."

I was born in Alabama, but I only lived there for a month when I'd done everything there was to do.

Adults are always asking kids what they want to be when they grow up because they're looking for ideas.

Democrats are the party that says government will make you smarter, taller, healthier; and remove the crabgrass from your lawn. Republicans are the party that says government doesn't work and then, when they get elected, go and prove it.

A husband is someone who, after taking the trash out, gives the impression that he just cleaned the whole house.

If you want someone who will eat whatever you put in front of him and will never say it's not quite as good as his mother's, get a dog.

Marriage is the triumph of imagination over intelligence.

A duck's quack doesn't echo. It's a mystery.

Democracy is a device that insures we shall be governed no better than we deserve.
                              -George Bernard Shaw

Why is our memory good enough to retain the least triviality, yet not good enough to remember how often we've told it to the same person?
                              -Larochefoucauld

IT'S A HARD LIFE IN TECHNICAL SUPPORT

Tech Support: Click on the My Computer icon on the left side of the screen.
Customer: Your left or my left?

Tech Support: Hello, how may I help you?
Customer: Hi…I can't print.
Tech Support: Okay. Please click on START.
Customer: Listen, pal, don't start getting technical with me. I'm not Bill Gates!

Customer: I can't seem to print in red.
Tech Support: Do you have a color printer?
Customer: Ahhhh …. Thank you.

Tech Support: Your password is the small letter "a" as in apple, a cap V as in Victor and the number 7.
Customer: Is that 7 in capital letters?

Customer: I'm having a problem printing.
Tech Support: Are you running it under Windows?
Customer: No, but the man next to me is by a window and his printer is working fine! Thanks for the tip!

Spent most of my life golfing. The rest I wasted.

Lynn Lavner says, "There are a number of mechanical devices which increase sexual arousal, particularly in women... among these is the Mercedes-Benz 500SL."

Did you ever notice? "The" and "IRS" put together spells "theirs."

If the world were a logical place, men would be the ones riding sidesaddle.

I'm single because I was born that way.
                                              –Mae West

A woman is incomplete until she is married. Then she's finished.

A woman inserted an ad in the local classifieds: "Husband Wanted."
Next day she received 100 letters. They all said the same thing: "You can have mine."

It's called golf because all the other four-letter words were taken.

When I woke up this morning, I had no wrinkles, the house was spotless, the garden absolutely lovely. And my grumpy husband looked quite handsome.
I don't think I'll ever put my glasses on again!

Sometimes I feel like throwing in the towel. But you know what that means:
MORE LAUNDRY.

At a cocktail party, one woman said to another, "Aren't you wearing your wedding ring on the wrong finger?"
"Yes, I am. I married the wrong man."

My friend said to me, "I never knew what true happiness was until I got married...and by then, it was too late."

First guy says, "My wife's an angel"
Second guy says, "You're lucky. Mine's still alive!"

If you want your spouse to listen and pay attention to every word you say...talk in your sleep.

Money is how talentless people keep score.

Just think...if it weren't for marriage, men would go through life thinking they had no faults at all.

A guy is out to dinner with his wife. He says, "So, what would you like for your birthday? A new car? Diamond earrings?"
She says: "I want a divorce."
He replies in shock: "I wasn't planning on spending that much!"

I don't want any yes-men around me. I want everybody to tell me the truth ...even if it costs them their jobs.
–Sam Goldwyn

Blessed is he who expects nothing, for he will never be disappointed.
–Jonathan Swift

Crime does not pay...as well as politics.
-Alfred E. Newman

I know Kung Fu, Karate, and 47 other dangerous words.
-Jo Ramos

The more I study religions, the more I am convinced that man has never worshipped anything but himself. –Sir Richard F. Burton

At a concert in Israel, Bono, lead singer for U2, asks the audience for some quiet. Then he starts to slowly clap his hands. Holding the audience in total silence, he says into the microphone: "I want you to think about something. Every time I clap my hands, a child in Africa dies."
A female voice comes from the audience: "Nu...so stop clapping!"

REMEMBER GRACIE ALLEN?

Smartness runs in my family. When I went to school I was so smart my teacher was in my class for five years.

When I was born I was so surprised I didn't talk for a year and a half.

This used to be a government of checks and balances. Now it's all checks and no balances.

I have the body of a god...Buddha.

A government agent came to investigate a small rancher in Missouri, to see if he was paying sufficient wages to his help. "I need a list of your employees and how much you pay them," he told the rancher.
"Well, there's my hired hand who's been here for three years. I pay him $200 a week plus free room and board.
"Then there's the mentally challenged worker. He puts in about 18 hours a day and does about 90% of the work. He makes about $10 a week and pays for his own room and board. I buy him a bottle of rye every Saturday to help him cope. Oh, and he sometimes sleeps with my wife."
"That's the guy I want to talk to," said the agent, "the mentally challenged one."
The rancher said, "That would be me."

"Researchers have discovered that chocolate produces some of the same reactions in the brain as marijuana. The researchers also discovered other similarities between the two, but can't remember what they are."
    -Matt Lauer on NBC's TODAY show

"It is wonderful to be here in the great state of Chicago."
    -former U.S. V.P. Dan Quayle.

DON'T YOU MISS ANDY ROONEY?

Andy Rooney always liked to begin with "I've learned..."

"...that the best classroom in the world is at the feet of an elderly person."

"...that when you're in love, it shows."

"...that you should never say no to a gift from a child."

"...that to ignore the facts does not change the facts."

"...that when you plan to get even with someone, you are only letting that person continue to hurt you."

"...that we should be glad that God doesn't give us everything we ask for."

"...that just one person saying to me, 'You've made my day,' makes my day."

"...that being kind is more important than being right."

FINALLY, MEN EXPLAINED

Handsome men are not nice.

Handsome men who are also nice are gay.

Men who are not so cute but are nice, have no money.

Men who are handsome and are nice and have money, think we're after their money.

Handsome, not-so-nice men who are somewhat heterosexual, don't think we're beautiful enough.

Men who think we are beautiful and are heterosexual, somewhat nice, with money...they're cowards.

Men who never make the first move automatically lose interest in us if we take the initiative.

Now, who the hell can understand men?

And they say women are difficult!

CAN YOU BELIEVE IT?

Police in Oakland, California spent two hours attempting to subdue a gunman who had barricaded himself inside his home. After firing ten tear gas canisters, police discovered that the man was standing beside them in the police line, shouting, "Please come out and give yourself up!"

A man walked into a Topeka, Kansas Kwik Stop and asked for all the money in the cash drawer. Apparently, the take was too small, so he tied up the store clerk and worked the counter himself for three hours until police showed up and grabbed him.

AT&T fired President John Walter after only nine months, saying he lacked intellectual leadership. He received a $26 million severance package. Perhaps it's not Walter who's lacking intelligence.

In Syracuse, NY, a man was arrested for trying to hold up a Bank of America without a weapon. He was using his thumb and forefinger as a pretend gun, but he forgot to put his hand in his pocket.

KALULUA is the South African airline with a sense of humor. Here's proof:

After a particularly rough landing during thunderstorms in the Karoo, a flight attendant announced: "Please take care when opening the overhead compartments because, after a landing like that, sure as hell everything has shifted."

Upon landing, the flight attendant said: "Please be sure to take all of your belongings. If you're going to leave anything behind, make sure it's something we'd like."

"Thank you for flying Kalula. We hope you enjoyed giving us the business as much as we enjoyed taking you for a ride."

"Ladies and gentlemen, we've reached cruising altitude and will be turning down the cabin lights. This is for your comfort and to enhance the appearance of your flight attendants."

"There may be 50 ways to leave your lover, but only four ways out of this airplane."

"Weather at our destination is 50 degrees with some broken clouds, but we'll try to have them fixed before we arrive. Thank you and remember, nobody loves you and your money like Kalula Airlines."

There is no assigned seating on Kalula. One day, the following announcement blared: "People, people, we're not picking out furniture here. Find a seat and get in it!"

As the plane landed and was coming to a stop at Durban Airport, a male voice came from the cockpit: "Whoa, big fella. WHOA!"

Heard from the intercom after a very hard landing: "That was quite a bump. I'm here to tell you that it wasn't the airline's fault, it wasn't the pilot's fault, it wasn't the flight attendant's fault. It was the asphalt!"

Arrival notice from the captain:
"We'd like to thank you folks for flying with us today. And the next time you get the insane urge to go blasting through the skies in a pressurized metal tube, we hope you'll think of Kalula Airways."

3 PAGES OF THE LOVABLE AND WISE BILL COSBY

A word to the wise ain't necessary – it's the stupid ones that need the advice.

Any man today who returns from work, sinks into a chair, and calls for his pipe is a man with an appetite for danger.

Always end the name of your child with a vowel, so that when you yell the name, it carries.

A new father quickly learns that his child invariably comes to the bathroom at precisely the times he's in there, as if he needed company. The only way for this father to be certain of bathroom privacy is to shave at the gas station.

Having a child is surely the most beautifully irrational act that two people in love can commit.

Fatherhood is pretending that the present you love most is soap-on-a-rope.

When you become senile, you won't know it.

I am certainly not an authority on love because there are no authorities on love, just those who've had luck and those who haven't.

I am proud to be an American. Because an American can eat anything on the face of this earth as long as he has two pieces of bread.

Every closed eye is not sleeping and every open eye is not seeing.

Even though your kids will consistently do the opposite of what you tell them to do, you have to keep loving them just as much.

Human beings are the only creatures on earth that let their kids come back home.

I don't know the key to success, but the key to failure is trying to please everybody.

There is no labor a person does that is undignified, if they do it right.

The past is a ghost, the future a dream, and all we ever have is now.

If the new American father feels bewildered and even defeated, let him take comfort from the fact that whatever he does in any fathering situation has a fifty percent chance of being right.

As I have discovered by examining my past, I started out as a child. Coincidentally, so did my brother.

My mother did not put all her eggs in one basket, so to speak; she gave me a younger brother named Russell who taught me what was meant by "survival of the fittest."

I guess the real reason that my wife and I had children is the same reason that Napoleon had for invading Russia. It seemed like a good idea at the time.

Civilization had too many rules for me, so I did my best to change them.

Decide that you want it more than you're afraid of it.

The only time my prayers are never answered is on the golf course.
		-Billy Graham

If you think it's hard to meet people, try picking up the wrong golf ball.
		-Jack Lemmon

Golf and sex are the only things you can enjoy without being good at them.

Harry opened the morning newspaper and was dumbfounded to read in the obituaries that he had died. He quickly phoned his best friend Herb. "Herb, did you see the paper? They're saying I died!" "Yes, I saw it," said Herb. "Where're you calling from?"

Three friends met weekly in a pub and one week, they each bought five tickets to the weeky raffle; and were delighted that each one of them had won a prize. Tom won a case of beer. Dick won a set of three fly swatters. And Harry won a nice toilet brush. The next week they discussed their winnings. Tom was happy. Dick was satisfied. But Harry said, "The toilet brush isn't so good. I think I'll go back to paper."

The bartender in a saloon noticed one fellow who came in every Saturday and ordered three mugs of ale. He sipped at each until they were all gone and then ordered three more.
Said the barman, "You could be sure of a cold drink if you order only one at a time, you know."
"Yes, I know. But let me explain. I have two brothers and we used to get together every week and have two mugs of ale. Now one is in Australia and one in Ireland. We made a vow that, every Saturday night, we'd still drink together. Right now, both my brothers have ordered their second drinks and we feel together."
This tradition continued for the better part of the year and then one Saturday, the fellow came in, ordered only two, then two more. The barman said, "I'm really sorry that one of your brothers died, man."
'Oh, no," said the fellow. "My brothers are fine. I just stopped drinking."

"That lowdown no good son of a bitch deserves to be kicked to death by a jackass. And I'm just the one to do it!"
-a Congressional candidate

The Samioffs were selling their house through an agent. He showed them his write-up for the papers.
"Is it really that nice?" asked the wife.
"Of course it is."
"Well we're not selling. It's too damn good to give up."

History explained...maybe.
Some archeologists in Israel found a slab of rock with five figures carved on it: a woman, a donkey, a shovel, a fish, a Star of David. After much study, the head of the expedition went on a lecture tour. The woman being first, he explained, showed that these people might have worshipped a goddess. The donkey was their beast of burden and the shovel showed that they knew how to make tools. The fish indicated that they knew how to get food from the sea and the Star of David was proof that they were a religious people. An old man in the front row of one of these lectures jumped up. "No, no," he said. "You were reading the slab left to right. Since this was obviously a group of Hebrews, they would read from right to left. "Here's what it really says: 'Holy mackerel, dig the ass on that babe!'"

THE FINAL WORD ON NUTRITION AND HEALTH

Japanese eat very little fat and suffer fewer heart attacks than the English.

Mexicans eat a lot of fat and suffer fewer heart attacks than the English.

Chinese drink very little red wine and suffer fewer heart attacks than the English.

Italians drink a lot of red wine and suffer fewer heart attacks than the English.

Germans drink a lot of beer and eat lots of sausages and fried potatoes and suffer fewer heart attacks than the English

As for French people, they're famous for their love of many glasses of wine and meals with endless courses, and they suffer fewer heart attacks than the English.

CONCLUSION: Eat and drink whatever you like.
Speaking English is apparently what kills you.

Psychiatry students were attending their first class on Emotional Extremes.
"Just to establish some parameters," said the professor to the student from New Jersey, "What is the opposite of joy?"
"Sadness," said the student.
"And the opposite of depression?" he asked the young lady from Missouri.
"Elation," she answered.
"And, you, sir," he said to the young man from Texas. "How about the opposite of woe?"
Said the Texan: "Sir, I believe that would be giddy-up."

A lonely frog phones the Psychic Hotline and asks what his future might hold.
His Personal Psychic Advisor tells him, "You are going to meet a beautiful young female who will want to know you inside and out."
The frog is thrilled. "This is great!" he croaks. "Where will I meet her? At a party?"
"No," says the psychic. "In biology class."

Flies spread illness. Keep yours zipped.

You can lead a cow upstairs...but not down.

DID YOU KNOW...?

The first couple to be shown in bed together on prime-time TV were Fred and Wilma Flintstone.

Men can read smaller print than women, but women hear better.

More Monopoly money is printed every year than real money.

Those San Francisco cable cars are the only mobile National Monuments in the U.S.

The first novel written on a typewriter: Tom Sawyer.

The youngest Pope was eleven years old.

Coca-Cola was originally green.

Intelligent people have more zinc and copper in their hair.

It is impossible to lick your elbow.

Conception occurs most often in December.

The sentence "the quick brown fox jumps over the lazy dog" uses every letter in our alphabet.

Debra Winger was the voice of E.T.

"I am" is the shortest complete sentence in the English language.

"Stewardesses" is the longest word that is typed with only the left hand.

There is no word in English that rhymes with month, orange, silver, and purple.

In the Middle Ages, the floor in your house was dirt—unless you were very wealthy—hence the saying "dirt poor."
The well-to-do had slate floors which would get slippery when wet and especially in winter.
So thresh was spread on the floor to keep people from falling down. As they added more and more, the thresh would start to slip outside when the door was opened. Then someone smart thought of putting a piece of wood at the entryway...or, in other words, a thresh hold.

During the Dark Ages, bread would be divided according to status. Peasants and servants got the burnt bottom of the loaf, the family got the middle, and guests were given the top, the upper crust.

Those with money were able to have plates made of pewter. Food with a high acid content made the lead leach into the food, making people very sick. This happened most often with tomatoes, so word went around that they were poisonous. People stopped eating tomatoes. It took 400 years for someone to try a tomato again.

Why is June the wedding month?
Most people took their yearly bath in May and were starting to smell a bit by June. Brides carried a bouquet of sweet smelling blossoms to hide body odor.

Lead cups used for ale or whiskey could make a person pass out for days. So they were laid out on the table while folks sat eating and drinking, waiting to see if the person would wake up. To this day, wakes are still held with eating and drinking in the same room with the corpse.

The only 15-letter word that can be spelled without repeating a letter is uncopyrightable.

Sherlock Holmes and Dr. Watson are camping. They pitch their tent and go to sleep. At some point during the night, Holmes awakens the doctor.
"Watson, look up at the sky and tell me what you see."
Watson says, "I see billions and billions of stars."
"True. And what do you deduce from that?"
"Well, if there are so many stars in the universe, then it stands to reason that somewhere out there, a planet like ours is circling a sun like ours; and there may very well be life like ours."
Holmes answered: "Watson, you idiot! It means that someone stole our tent!"

What separates "60 Minutes" from every other show on television? No theme music.

100% of all lottery winners gain weight.

40% of all people who are invited into your home snoop in your medicine cabinet.

We used to hiss the villain. Now we buy his book.

Parents don't care about justice, they just want peace and quiet.

I'm on a seafood diet.
I see food and I eat it.

About a third of Americans say they do this while sitting on the toilet.
Flush.

What do bullet-proof vests, fire escapes, windshield wipers and laser printers all have in common?
They were all invented by women.

This stimulates 29 muscles and chemicals causing relaxation. Women seem to like it light and frequent. Men like it more strenuous. What is it?
A kiss.

There are more collect calls made on this day than any other day of the year.
Father's Day

The Pope and the Rabbi

Many years ago, the Pope decided that all Jews had to leave Rome. This caused a big uproar in the Jewish community and the peace of the city was threatened. One of the Cardinals suggested that the Pope have a religious debate with the chief Rabbi of Rome and so it was decided.

The Rabbi's Latin was almost non-existent and the Pope's Hebrew was not very good either. So, when the day of the great debate came, the Pope and the Rabbi sat opposite each other in one of the great Roman piazzas, without a common language. They looked at each other for a full minute, when the Pope raised his hand and showed three fingers. The Rabbi raised one finger in response. The Pope waved his finger in a circle around his head and the Rabbi's answer was to point one finger to the ground. The Pope pulled out a wafer and a glass of wine. The Rabbi pulled out an apple. At which the Pope stood and said, "I give up. This man is too smart. The Jews can stay."

Later the Pope explained, "I held three fingers to represent the Trinity. He held one finger to remind me we worship one God.

I showed the wine and wafer to show that God absolves us of sin and he pulled out an apple to remind me of original sin. He had an answer for everything."

Meanwhile, the Jewish community gathered around the Rabbi, demanding to know what happened.

"Well," said the rabbi, "First he told me the Jews had three days to get out of Rome. I told him that not one of us was leaving. Then he signaled that this whole city would be cleared of Jews and I let him know we were staying right here."

"And then?"

"I'm not sure," said the rabbi. "He took out his lunch and I took out mine."

Each king in a deck of playing cards represents a great king from history.
Clubs – Alexander the Great
Diamonds -- Julius Caesar
Hearts – Charlemagne
Spades – King David

If you fool some of the people all of the time and all of the people some of the time, don't worry. Someone else will fool the rest of them.

In very Olde England, they started to run out of land in which to bury their dead. So, they would dig up coffins, take the bones to a house and re-use the grave. They discovered that in a great many cases, the inside of the coffin had deep scratch marks; and they realized they had been burying people while they were still alive! Someone thought to tie a string on the corpse's wrist and lead it through the coffin and up through the ground and tie it to a bell. Someone would have to sit up out in the graveyard all night to listen for the bell. Hence, on the "graveyard shift" they would know that someone was "saved by the bell" or was a "dead ringer."

The three most valuable brand names on earth are MARLBORO, COCA-COLA, and BUDWEISER...in that order.

Average life span of a major-league baseball: seven pitches.

Clans of long ago that wanted to get rid of certain people without killing them, would burn down their houses. From which we get the expression "to get fired."

If men can run the world, why can't they stop wearing neckties? How intelligent is it to start the day by tying a little noose around your neck?
-Linda Ellerbee

In politics, if you want something said, ask a man; if you want anything done, ask a woman.   -Margaret Thatcher

I base most of my fashion sense on what doesn't itch.   -Gilda Radner

Sometimes I wonder if men and women really suit each other. Perhaps they should live next door and just visit now and then.
-Katherine Hepburn

Any girl can be glamorous. All you have to do is stand still and look stupid.
–Hedy Lamarr

I never married because there was no need. I have a dog which growls every morning, a parrot which swears all afternoon and a cat that comes home late at night.
-Marie Corelli

Man invented language for complaining.

A guest in a seaside hotel breakfast room called over the head waiter one morning. "I'd like two boiled eggs, one of them undercooked and runny, the other overcooked so that it's tough and hard to cut. Also, grilled bacon that has been left on the plate to get cold; burnt toast; butter straight out of the fridge so that it's impossible to spread, and a pot of very weak coffee, lukewarm."
"That's a complicated order," said the bewildered waiter. "It might be difficult."
Said the guest, "Oh, really? But that's exactly what you gave me yesterday."

A prosperous farmer was retiring and wanted to get rid of his animals. He decided to give a horse to homes where the man is the boss; and to homes run by women, a chicken. On one street, he spotted a couple gardening. "Who's the boss around here?" he asked.
"I am," said the husband.
"I have a black horse and a brown horse I'd like to give away. Which one would you like?" The man said, "The black one."
"No, no, get the brown one," said his wife.
"Here's your chicken," said the farmer.

A city dude drove his car into a ditch in a very rural area. Luckily, he was spotted by a farmer who came to help with a big strong-looking horse named Buddy. He hitched Buddy to the car and yelled, "Pull, Nellie, Pull!" Buddy didn't respond.
Once more, the farmer yelled. "Pull, Coco, pull!" Nothing happened.
Then he said nonchalantly, "Okay, Buddy, pull!" The horse easily dragged the car out of the ditch.
The motorist was most appreciative and also curious. He asked the farmer why he called the horse by three different names.
The farmer said: "Oh, Buddy is blind, and if he thought he was the only one pulling, he wouldn't even try!"

A woman has a heart attack; and in the hospital has a near-death experience and sees God. God says she has another 25 years. She figures why not make the most of it? So she has a lot of plastic surgery and changes her hair color. She walks out of the salon and is killed by a speeding car.
She complains to God: "You said I had 25 more years!"
God says: "Sorry. I didn't recognize you."

A young engineer was leaving the office after regular closing time and found the CEO standing in front of a shredder with a piece of paper in his hand and a bewildered look on his face.

"Listen," said the CEO, "this is a very sensitive and important document and my secretary has left. Can you make this machine work?"

"Certainly," said the young woman. She turned on the machine, inserted the paper, and pressed the START button.

"Excellent, excellent!" said her boss, as the paper disappeared into the machine. "I just need one copy."

LESSON: Never, never, <u>ever</u> assume that your boss knows what he's doing.

I hate people who say, "He's a nice person once you get to know him."
They might as well just say, "He's a dickhead, but you'll get used to it."

On the internet, you can be anything you want. It's strange that so many people choose to be stupid.

Take my advice—I'm not using it.

By Woody Allen: "In my next life, I want to live my life backwards. You start out dead and get that out of the way. Then you wake up in an old people's home feeling better every day. You get kicked out for being too healthy, go collect your pension, and then when you start work, you get a gold watch and a party on your first day. You work for 40 years until you're young enough to enjoy your retirement. You party, drink alcohol, and are generally promiscuous, then you are ready for high school. You then go to primary school, you become a kid, you play. You have no responsibilities. You become a baby until you are born. And then you spend your last nine months floating in luxurious spa-like conditions with central heating and room service on tap, larger quarters every day and then, voila! You finish off as an orgasm.

NASA's robot Curiosity landed on Mars. Early pictures show no signs of ESPN, beer, or porn. This makes it very clear that men are NOT from Mars.

I used to wish I could read minds. Then I got a Facebook account and I'm over it.

As I grow older, I've learned that pleasing everyone is impossible, but pissing everyone off is a piece of cake.

Three guys fishing on a lake were visited by an angel.
The angel said, "What can I do for you gentlemen? I have a little time down here."
One man said he'd been suffering back pain since his time in the Army. The angel touched his back and the pain disappeared.
The second guy asked if the angel could do anything about his deteriorating vision. The angel smiled, removed the man's glasses, and threw them in the lake. Instantly, he could see everything very clearly.
When the angel turned to the third fisherman, he put out his hands defensively. "Don't touch me!" he cried. "I'm on a disability pension!"

Crazy Laws in Baltimore, Maryland
You may not grow thistles in your yard.
It's illegal to take a lion to the movies.
It's illegal to throw bales of hay from a second-story window within city limits.
It's a violation of city code to sell chicks or ducklings within one week of Easter.

A woman was in a terrible automobile accident and needed a great deal of healthy skin to remake her face. She was a very slender woman without a lot of extra skin. Her husband, a husky man, volunteered his own skin.

After much consultation, it was decided that the smooth skin on his buttocks would be the best; and all concerned were sworn to secrecy. After all, the whole thing was very delicate in nature.

The skin grafts took beautifully and everyone was astounded at the woman's new beauty. She looked younger and more glowing than she ever had. Needless to say, she was a happy woman.

One day, when she was alone with her husband, she gave him a big kiss, overcome with emotion.

"Darling, I know that you suffered while your skin was growing back. I know that the pain was terrible. I cannot say how grateful I am to you for your sacrifice.

"There is no way I could ever repay you for what you did."

Smiling, he replied,

"I get all the thanks I need every time I see your mother kiss you on the cheek."

A woman awoke during the night and saw that her husband was not in bed. She put on her robe and went downstairs, finding him sitting at the kitchen table, a glass of scotch in front of him. He seemed to be in deep thought, just staring into space. She saw him wipe what might be a tear from one eye and take a sip of his scotch.
"What's the matter, dear?" she asked. "What are you doing down here so late?"
"Do you remember when we were first dating and you were only sixteen?"
"Yes, I remember."
"And your father caught us in the back seat of my car, making love?"
Softly: "Of course I do."
"Do you remember when he threatened me and said, 'Either you marry my daughter or spend twenty years in jail?'"
"Yes, I do," she said.
He wiped another tear away and said, "You know ... I would have gotten out today."

Once my divorce was final, I went to the DMV to change to my maiden name on my license. "Change of address, too?" asked the clerk. I told her, No. "Oh, good," she said. "You got the house."

I hate all this terrorist business. I miss the days when you could look at an unattended bag on a train or in an airport and think to yourself, I'm going to take that.

My husband bought me a mood ring. When I'm in a good mood it, turns aqua. When I'm in a bad mood, it leaves a red mark on his forehead.

After a long talk with the estranged husband, the lawyer reported, "Mrs. Jones, I've succeeded in making a settlement that is extremely fair to both of you."
"Fair to both!" she shouted. "I could have done that myself! What do you think I hired a lawyer for?"

A divorcing couple is having trouble deciding upon custody of their two children.
The mother tells the judge that, since she carried and gave birth to them, she should retain custody of them.
The father also wants custody and the judge asks for his justification.
"Your Honor, when I put a dollar in the Coke machine and a Coke comes out, does it belong to the machine or to me?"

She married him because he was such a strong man.
She divorced him because he was so domineering.

He married her because she was so petite and cute.
He divorced her because she was too helpless.

She married him because "he'll provide us with a good living."
She divorced him because "all he thinks about is business."

He married her because she reminded him of his mother.
He divorced her because she's becoming more and more like his mother every day.

She married him because he was romantic.
She divorced him because he was shiftless.

He married her because she was so steady.
He divorced her because she was so boring.

They married each other for their different viewpoints...same reason for their divorce.

Sitting by her window in the convent, Sister Barbara opened a letter from home one evening. Inside was a $100 bill her parents had sent her.

She smiled at the gesture. Glancing out the window, she saw a shabbily dressed stranger leaning against a lamppost. Quickly, she wrote: "Don't despair. Sister Barbara" on a piece of paper, folded the paper around the $100 bill, got the man's attention, and tossed the bundle out the window to him. The stranger picked it up looking puzzled, tipped his baseball cap to her, and left. The next day, Sister Barbara was told that there was a man at the front door, insisting that he see her.

She went downstairs, and there he was again, the stranger, waiting.

Without a word, he handed her a huge wad of $100 bills. "What's this?" she asked.

"That's the $8,000 you got coming, Sister," he replied.

"Don't Despair paid 80 to one."

The boss was exasperated. His new secretary never answered the phone. "Why not?" he asked. She explained: "Well, nine times out of ten it's for you."

THE NEW HUSBAND STORE

A store selling new husbands has just opened. It has special instructions. You may visit the store ONLY ONCE. There are six floors and the value of the products increase as you go up. You may choose from any floor, or keep going up; but you cannot go back down except to exit the building.

A woman goes to the Husband Store and gets on the escalator.

FLOOR ONE: these men have jobs. Okay, she thinks, but let's see what's next.

FLOOR TWO: these men have jobs and love kids. "Nice," she mutters aloud, "but I think I want more."

FLOOR THREE: these men have jobs, love kids, and are very handsome. Lovely, she thinks, but what _else_ is there?

FLOOR FOUR: these men have jobs, love kids, are drop-dead handsome and help with housework. Wow! she thinks; but continues on up to the next level.

FLOOR FIVE; these men have jobs, love kids, are gorgeous, help with housework, and have a strong romantic streak. She is so tempted; but there must be more, right?

So she continues up to the next floor.
FLOOR SIX: you are Visitor #31,485,045 to this floor. There are no men on this floor, which exists solely as proof that women are impossible to please. Thank you for visiting the Husband Store and turn left to take the escalator down to the exit.

THE NEW WIFE STORE

To avoid gender bias charges, another store was opened across the street where men could choose a wife. The same rules applied.
FLOOR ONE: women that love sex.
FLOOR TWO: women that love sex, have money, and like to drink beer.
The third, fourth, fifth, and sixth floors have never been visited.

* * * *   * * * *

ANDY ROONEY on prisons: Did you know it costs forty-thousand dollars a year to house each prisoner? Jeez, for 40,000 bucks apiece, I'll take a few prisoners into my house. I live in Los Angeles; I already have bars on the windows.

ANDY ROONEY on ads in your bills: Have you noticed that they put ads in with your bills now? Like bills aren't distasteful enough, they have to stuff in junk mail. I get back at them. I put garbage in with my payment. Coffee grounds, apple skins...I put them in before I mail it. I write, "Could you throw this away for me? Thank you."

ANDY ROONEY on phone-in polls: You know those shows where people call in and vote on different issues? Did you ever notice there's always like 18% "I don't know." It costs 90 cents to call up and vote and they're voting "I don't know." "Honey, I feel very strongly about this. Give me the phone." (Into the phone) "I DON'T KNOW!" Sometimes you have to stand up for what you believe you're not sure about. This guy probably calls up phone sex girls for $2.95, to say "I'm not in the mood."

ANDY ROONEY on euphemisms: My wife's from the Midwest. Very nice people. They say, "For Cripe's sake!" Who would that be? Jesus Cripes? The son of Gosh of the church of Holy Moly? I'm not making fun of it.
You think I want to go to Heck?

A young man was hired by a huge international firm as a trainee. On his first day, he called the dining room and said, "Bring me hot coffee and make it quick!" The voice from the other end said, "You idiot, you punched in the wrong number. Do you know who you're talking to?"
"No," said the trainee.
"I'm the Managing Director of the company!"
"Oh, really? And do you know who <u>you're</u> talking to?"
"No!"
"Good," replied the trainee and hung up.

A blonde made several attempts to sell her old car. The car had 240,000 miles on it and that was a problem. She discussed this with a friend. The friend said, "I know a way you can sell that car, but it's not legal,"
"I don't care," declared the blonde.
"Okay, here's the name and address of a guy who owns this repair shop. He'll turn back the mileage on your car to 40,000 miles. Then it should be easy to sell."
A month later, they happened to meet. "Did you sell your car?" asked the friend.
"Hell, no!" said the blonde, "It's got only 40,000 miles on it!"

LIFE'S DEMERIT SYSTEM FOR MEN
Do something she likes, you get points.
Do something she doesn't like, you get points subtracted.
You get no points for something she expects. Sorry, that's how the game is played..

You make the bed. (+1)
You make the bed but forget the fancy pillows. (-10)
You throw the bedspread over rumpled sheets. (-3)

You go out to buy her what she wants. (+5) In the rain. (+8). But return with beer. (-5)

You check out a nighttime noise. (+1)
You check out a nighttime noise and it's nothing. (0) or it's something. (+5)
You pummel it with an iron rod. (+10)
It's her new Schnauzer. (-20)

You take her out to dinner for her birthday. (+2) And it's not a sports bar. (+3) Okay, it's a sports bar. (-3) And it's all-you-can-eat night. (-3) And your face gets painted the colors of your favorite team. (-10)

The Ultimate Bathroom Joke Book

You stay by her side for the entire party. (+1) You stay by her side, but soon you leave to chat with an old school friend. (-2) Named Tina. (-10) Who is a dancer. (-10) And who has breast implants. (-40)

You take her to a movie. (+1) It's a movie she likes. (+5) And it's a movie you hate. (+6) You take her to a movie you like. (-2) It's called "Death Cop." (-3) You said it was a foreign film about orphans. (-15)

You develop a pot belly. (-15) You exercise. (+10) You resort to baggy jeans and large Hawaiian shirts. (-30) You say, "So what? You have one, too." (-80)

She asks, "Do I look fat to you?" (-5) (Yes, you lose points even before you answer.) You hesitate before responding. (-10) You Finally ask, "Where?" (-35) Or you say anything else. (-20)

When she wants to discuss a problem, you listen with a concerned expression. (+2) For over 30 minutes. (+50) Without sneaking looks at the TV. (+500) And then she realizes you have fallen asleep. (-4,000)

Nine exuberant blondes come charging into a bar, order five bottles of champagne and ten glasses and carry it all to a table. The corks are popped, the glasses filled, and they begin chanting, "51 days! 51 days! 51 days!" and giving each other high fives.
After a few minutes, a tenth blonde comes in and balances a framed picture against one of the bottles. They all begin dancing around the table, shouting "51 days! 51 days!"
Finally, the bartender can stand it no longer. He comes over and says, "What's all the celebrating about?"
The blonde who brought in the pictures says, "You know, everyone thinks blondes are dumb and they make fun of us. So we decided to set them straight. Ten of us got together and bought a jigsaw puzzle, and put it together.
"The side of the box said 2 to 4 years, but we put it together in 51 days!"

The same clutter that fills a one-car garage can also fill a two-car garage.

Leftovers expand to fill all available containers ... plus one.

ANONYMOUS SPORTS QUOTES
Names have been removed to protect everyone's reputation

"Nobody in football should be called a genius. A genius is, like, Norman Einstein."

"You guys pair up in groups of three, then line up in a circle."

"He's a guy who gets up at six o'clock in the morning regardless of what time it is."

"I'm going to graduate on time, no matter how long it takes."

"You guys line up alphabetically by height."

"We can't win at home. We can't win on the road.
"As general manager, I just can't figure out where else to play."

"I've won at every level except college and pro."

"My sister's expecting a baby and I don't know if I'm going to be an uncle or an aunt."

OFFICE WISDOM

If you do a good job and work hard, you may get a job with a better company someday.

The light at the end of the tunnel has been turned off due to budget cuts.

Sure, you may not like working here. But we pay your rent.

Rome did not create a great empire by having meetings. They did it by killing all those who opposed them.

A person who smiles in the face of adversity probably has a scapegoat.

Abandon all hope, ye who enter here.

If at first you don't succeed ... try management.

It's only unethical if you get caught.

We make great money! We have great benefits! We do no work! We're Union!

The manager of the company was a woman and she was known to be tough. This day, she was interviewing a new employee. "What's your name?" "George."
She scowled. "Look, Georgie, I don't know what feel-good company you worked for last, but in this office, there are no first names. I call all my workers by their last name: Shapiro, O'Connell, Jones, and so forth. You got that?" The man nodded. "Okay, let's start again. What's your name?" "Darling. My full name is George Darling." "Okay, George, so my next question is..."

A mother and her small daughter were visiting New York City for the first time. The mother hailed a cab and fielded all the child's questions. When the girl asked, "Who are all those ladies wearing shorts in the cold?" her mother said, "Oh, they're waiting for their husbands."
The cabbie snarled, "Aw, c'mon, lady, tell her the truth! They're hookers, plain and simple."
After a brief silence, the child said, "Do those ladies have any kids?"
"Of course," said her mother. "Where do you think cabbies come from?"

An atheist is swimming in the ocean and is a long way from his boat, when he sees that horrible sight: the fin of a shark, and it's heading right for him! He swims as fast as he can, but he knows he'll never make it to the boat. "God, oh God," he screams, "please save me!"

In an instant, the entire scene stops, frozen in time, and a bright light shines down from above.

A huge voice says, "You do not believe in me, so why do you expect me to help you?"

"It's true that I am not a believer, but... but could you make the shark a believer?" asks the terrified man, thinking that a saved shark would never attack another being.

"As you wish."

The light retracts, the water moves again and the shark's jaws begin to close down on him when suddenly the shark stops short and pulls back.

Shocked, the man looks on as the huge beast closes its eyes, bows its head and intones, "Thank you, Lord, for this food which I am about to receive."

We all have to go sometime. Why don't you go now?

Q & A

Q: What's the one thing that all men at singles bars have in common?
A: They're married.

Q: What do you call a woman who knows where her husband is every night?
A: A widow.

Q: Why is it so difficult to find men who are sensitive, caring and good-looking?
A: They already have boyfriends.

Q: How many honest, intelligent, caring men in the world does it take to wash dishes?
A: Both of them.

Q: Why did the man cross the road?
A: He heard the chicken was a slut.

Q: Why don't women blink during foreplay?
A: They don't have time.

Q: Why does it take millions of sperm to fertilize one egg?
A: They won't stop and ask for directions.

A most unusual funeral procession made its slow way through our town. A long black hearse was followed by a second long black hearse. Behind the second hearse walked a woman dressed in black with a pit bull on a leash. And a short distance behind her, snaked a line of perhaps 200 women walking single file.

I was so curious that I respectfully approached the woman walking the dog and said, "I am so sorry for your loss and I hate to disturb you at such a time; but I have never seen a funeral procession like this one. Whose funeral is it?"

"My husband's," was the answer.

"What happened to him?"

"My dog attacked and killed him."

I couldn't help asking, "But who is in the second hearse?"

"My mother-in-law. She tried to help my husband and the dog turned on her."

I stared deeply into this woman's eyes. After a moment of silence, I said, "Can I borrow the dog?"

Her answer: "Get in line."

Out of body. Back in 5 minutes.

I feel like a million...only one at a time.

A woman went to an attorney to ask about a divorce. "What grounds do you have?" asked the lawyer.
"About six acres."
"No, I don't think you quite understand. Let me rephrase. Do you have a grudge?"
"No, just a parking space."
"I'll try again. Does your husband beat you?" "No, I'm always up an hour before him." The lawyer could see he was getting nowhere fast. "Madam, are you sure you want a divorce?" "I'm not the one who wants the divorce," said the client. "My husband does. He claims we don't communicate."

Eleven people, ten men and a woman, were hanging on a rope under a helicopter. The rope was strong enough only for ten people, so one of them had to go. They couldn't decide which one, but then the woman said she would voluntarily let go since she was a woman and accustomed to giving up everything for her husband and her children, and actually for men in general.
As soon as she finished speaking, the men all enthusiastically clapped.

"Honey," said the husband, "I've invited Mark over for supper."
"Without asking me first? The house is a mess, I haven't been shopping, and I was planning to make eggs and bacon tonight!"
"I know that," said the husband.
"Then why in the world did you invite him?"
"The poor sucker's thinking of getting married!"

An efficiency expert concluded his lecture with a note of caution. "You don't want to try these techniques at home."
"Why not?" asked someone in the audience.
"I watched my wife's routine at breakfast for several years," said the expert. "She made a whole lot of trips between the fridge and the table and the stove and the fridge, usually carrying just one item at a time. So one day I said to her, "Honey, why don't you try putting several things at once on a tray?"
"And did that save time?"
"Actually, yes," replied the expert. "It used to take her twenty minutes to make breakfast. Now I do it in seven."

Things only seem to be lost. They're waiting for you in next week.

A WOMAN'S PRAYER

I pray for Wisdom,
To understand a man;
Love, to forgive his faults;
Patience, for his moods.
Because if I pray for Strength,
I just might beat him to death!

After his divorce, Mr. Jones realized that poker isn't the only game that starts with holding hands and ends with a staggering financial loss.

New Life Rule: Ladies, leave your eyebrows alone. Here's how much men care about them: Do you have two of them?
Okay, then, we're done.

Another New Life Rule: There's no such thing as flavored water. I know, I know. There's a whole aisle of this stuff at the supermarket. It's still water, but without that watery taste.
Sorry, but flavored water is called a soft drink. Want some flavored water? Pour some scotch over ice and let it melt. There's your flavored water.

A boy asked his father, "Dad, what's the difference between 'potentially' and 'realistically?'"

His father thought for a moment, then said: "Go ask your mother if she would sleep with Brad Pitt for a million dollars. Next, ask your sister the same thing and, last, ask your brother if he would sleep with Brad Pitt for a million dollars. Come back and tell me what you learn from their answers."

The boy asked his mother, "Would you sleep with Brad Pitt for a million dollars?"

She said, "Of course! We could really use that money to fix up the house and send you kids to a great university!"

The boy then went to his sister and asked her. "Are you kidding me?" said his sister. "I LOVE Brad Pitt, and I'd sleep with him in a heartbeat! What a question!"

The boy then asked his brother; and his brother said, "Yeah, I would. Do you realize what a million bucks would buy?"

The boy went back to his father. "I know the meaning of both words now, Dad. 'Potentially,' you and I are sitting on three million dollars. But, 'realistically,' we're living with two hookers and a future congressman."

NEW CONSOLIDATIONS IN BUSINESS

Hale Business Systems, Mary Kay Cosmetics, Fuller Brush, and W. R. Grace Co. will merge and become Hale, Mary, Fuller Grace.

Polygram Records, Warner Brothers and Ritz Crackers join forces and become Poly Warner Cracker.

3M will merge with Goodyear and morph into MMMGood.

Zippo Manufacturing, Aurdi Motors, Dofasco and Dakota Mining will merge into ZipAudiDoDa.

Fairchild publications and Honeywell electronics will become Fairwell Honeychild.

Grey Poupon mustard and Docker pants are expected to merge into Poupon Pants.

Knotts Berry Farms and the National Organization of Women will be known as Knott NOW.

POLITICIANS AS USUAL

These true stories come from a DC ticket agent.

A Congresswoman from New England asked for an aisle seat so her hair wouldn't get messed up by being next to the window...this is a plane we're talking about.

I got a call from a Congressman's aide, who said he wanted to go to Cape Town. I was surprised and started to explain the length of the flight and the passport information. He interrupted me with, "I'm not trying to make you look stupid, but Cape Town is in Massachusetts." Without trying to make him look stupid, I calmly explained, "Cape Cod is in Massachusetts. Cape Town is in South Africa." His response was to hang up.

A senior Congressman called, furious about a Florida package we did for him. I asked what was wrong with the vacation in Orlando. He said he was expecting an ocean- view room.
I explained that's not possible, since Orlando is in the middle of the state.

A Congresswoman from the middle of the country called last week. She wanted to know how it was possible that a flight from Detroit could leave at 8:30 AM and get to Chicago at 8:33 AM. I explained that Michigan is an hour ahead of Illinois, but she couldn't get the concept of time zones. Finally, I told her the plane went really fast and she bought that.

An aide for an East Coast Senator called to inquire about a trip package to Hawaii. When we had finished our discussion, she asked, "Would it be cheaper to fly to California and then take the train to Hawaii?"

A Congresswoman called and said, "I need to fly to Pepsi-Cola, Florida. Do I have to get on one of those little computer planes?" I asked if she meant fly to Pensacola on a commuter plane. And she said, "Yeah, whatever, smarty!"

A Congressman called with questions about a trip to China. After a lengthy discussion about passports, I reminded him that he needed a visa. "Oh, no, I don't. They've always accepted my American Express."

POLITICS AS USUAL

I offer my opponents a bargain: if they will stop telling lies about me I will stop telling the truth about them.   -Adlai Stevenson

Don't vote. It only encourages them.

Those who are too smart to engage in politics are punished by being governed by those who are dumber.   -Plato

We hang the petty thieves and appoint the really big ones to public office.   –Aesop

Politics is the same all over. Those in office promise to build a bridge even where there is no river.   -Nikita Khrushchev

Politicians, when they see light at the end of the tunnel, go out and buy more tunnel.

Politicians get votes from the poor and campaign funds from the rich, by promising to protect each from the other.

Politician: he'll double-cross that bridge when he comes to it.

A prisoner gets a letter from his wife.
"Dear husband, I have decided to plant tomatoes in the back garden. When should I put them in?"
The husband, knowing that all his mail is read by the guards, answers:
"Dear wife, whatever you do, don't touch the back garden. The money is buried there."
A week or so later, the prisoner receives another letter from his wife.
"Dear husband, You wouldn't believe what happened. A group of men came to the house with shovels and they dug up the entire back garden."
The prisoner wrote back:
"My dear wife, now you can plant the tomatoes."

While creating woman, God promised Adam that he would love this new creation and that good, obedient, sexy women would be found in all corners of the world.
Then She smiled and made the earth round.

Person One: You say your phone works underwater?
Person Two: Yes, when it's wringing wet.

DAMNING WITH VERY FAINT PRAISE

He would be out of his depth in a parking lot puddle.

This employee should go far and the sooner the better.

If you see two women talking and one is bored, she's the other one.

When his IQ reaches 50, he should sell.

A prime candidate for natural de-selection.

Gates are down, lights are flashing, but the train ain't coming.

She has two brains. One is lost and the other is out looking for it.

This person is depriving a village somewhere of its idiot.

When she opens her mouth, it's only to change feet.

He's been working too much with glue!

He works well when under constant supervision and cornered like a rat in a trap.

His men would follow him anywhere, but only out of morbid curiosity.

I would not allow this girl to breed.

She sets low personal standards and then consistently fails to achieve them.

This young man has delusions of adequacy.

This person is really not so much of a has-been, but more of a definite won't-be.

She doesn't have ulcers but certainly is a carrier.

He has a knack for making strangers immediately.

She would argue with a signpost.

He brings a lot of joy when he leaves the room.

Donated his brain to science before using it.

Since light travels faster than sound, some people appear to be bright until you hear them speak.

Take a lesson from the weather. It pays absolutely no attention to criticism.

Two blondes find three hand grenades and they decide to take them to the nearest police station.
One asked, "What if one explodes before we get there?"
Said the other: "We'll lie and say we found only two."

If the rich could hire other people to die for them, the poor could make a wonderful living.
                                        -Yiddish proverb

Andy Rooney said: My grandmother has a bumper sticker on her car that says "Sexy Senior Citizen." You don't want to think of your grandmother that way, do you? Out entering wet shawl contests. Makes you wonder where she got that dollar she gave you for your birthday.

Immigration is the sincerest form of flattery.

A hurricane in the Caribbean capsized a big beautiful yacht. There were only two survivors, the owner of the yacht and the steward. They managed to swim together to a nearby small deserted island.
The steward, a young man, was very upset and nearly hysterical. He moaned that they were surely doomed. His boss, on the other hand, seemed completely calm and was relaxed, leaning against a palm tree.
"How can you be so calm?" the young man cried. "Nobody will ever find us!"
"Oh yes, they will," said the yacht owner. "I give to two major charities and every year, I increase my donation by $500,000."
"So what?"
"Well, it's fundraising time right about now. I assure you, they will find me!"

Jim had an awful day fishing, so he stopped at the seafood store and said, "I'd like four catfish and please throw them at me."
"Why?" asked the counterman.
"So my wife will think I caught them."
"Then I suggest you take the flounder," said the counterman. "Your wife was around earlier today and said that's the fish she'd like to make for dinner tonight."

WARNING: The consumption of alcohol may lead you to believe that your ex-lovers are dying for you to telephone them at four in the morning.

He does not have a beer gut; he has developed a liquid grain storage facility.

He is not shy and quiet; he is a conversational minimalist.

She is not stupid; she suffers from minimal cranial development.

She does not get lost; she discovers alternative destinations.

Q: What do you mean by coming home half drunk?
A: It's not my fault. I ran out of money.

HE: Let's go out and have some fun tonight.
SHE: Okay, but if you get home before I do, leave the hall light on.

If crocodile skin makes shoes and bags, what does a banana skin make?
SLIPPERS.

A cop pulled a guy over for speeding.
"License and registration, please," he said.
Driver: Sorry, I don't have a license. It was suspended after my third DUI."
Cop: "Let me see the registration, sir."
Driver: "It's not in this vehicle. I stole this vehicle." Cop: "You're telling me this is a stolen car?" Driver: "That's right. But, on second thought, maybe I did see the registration in the glove box when I put my pistol in there." Cop: "So there's a gun in the glove box." Driver: "Yeah. I put it there after I shot the owner of this car and put his body in the trunk."
Cop: "THERE'S A BODY IN THE TRUNK?"
Driver: "Sure thing."
The officer now called his Captain and within minutes, they were surrounded by police. The Captain proceeded to go through the same line of questioning, only this time, the driver produced his license and the proper registration. There was no gun in the glove box and no body in the trunk.
The Captain said, "What's going on here? The officer who pulled you over told us you said you'd stolen this car, shot the owner, and put his body in the trunk."
"And I'll bet he said I was speeding, too!"

An old lady was a devout Christian. Often, she would stand on her front porch and shout, "PRAISE THE LORD!" Next to her lived an atheist and her shouting drove him nuts. One day, she stood on her porch and shouted: "I am hungry, oh Lord!" The next morning there were two bags of food on the porch. "PRAISE THE LORD! HE HAS FED ME!" The atheist came out and said, "There is no God. I bought those groceries for you!" The lady raised her hands upward and cried, "Praise the Lord! Not only did he feed me, but he made the devil pay for the food!"

Last week, a passenger heading for the British Museum in London leaned over and tapped the driver lightly on the shoulder to get his attention.
The driver screamed and lost control of the cab. For a moment, nothing was said. Then the driver apologized profusely. "I'm so sorry," he said, "but you scared the living daylights out of me."
The shaken passenger said, "I didn't realize a light tap like that could scare anyone."
"I must apologize," said the driver. "This is my first day driving a cab.
I've been driving a hearse for 25 years."

FINDING THE RIGHT PERSON FOR THE JOB

Put about 100 bricks in a closed room with one open window. Then send two or three candidates into the room and lock the door. Leave them alone for six hours, then come back and analyze the situation:
- If they're counting the bricks, put them into the Accounts Department.
- If they're recounting them, put them into Auditing.
- If the bricks are all over the place, put them into Engineering.
- If they are sleeping, put them into Security.
- If they're arranging the bricks in some strange order, put them in Planning.
- If they're throwing the bricks at each other, put them into Operations.
- If they are sitting idle, put them into Human Resources.
- It they're staring out of the window, put them in Strategic Planning.
- If they've left, put them in Marketing.
- If they are talking to each other and not a single brick has been touched...

Congratulate them and put them into Top Management.

Not wit, just wisdom: There is an old pub in London that used to have a gallows next door. The horse-drawn dray holding the prisoner would stop at the pub and ask him if he wanted one last drink.
If he said yes, it was "One for the Road." If he declined, he was "On the Wagon."

An extremely modest man was in the hospital for a series of tests, the last of which had upset his stomach terribly. After several false alarm trips to the bathroom, he suddenly filled his bed with diarrhea and was so embarrassed, he hardly knew what to do. In a complete panic, he gathered up his bed sheets and threw them out of the window. A drunk was walking by when the sheets landed on him.
He began to yell and curse, tussling with the sheets trying to get untangled and ended up with the pile of soiled sheets at his feet.
A hospital security guard who had seen most of the incident, walked up and said, "What the heck is going on here?"
The drunk, still staring in amazement at the messy pile of sheets, said:
"I think I just beat the shit out of a ghost."

KIDS AND MORE KIDS

The Ultimate Bathroom Joke Book

My young grandson called me the other day to wish me happy birthday. He asked me how old I was, and I told him, 75. He was quiet for a moment, and then he asked, "Did you start at one?"

After putting her grandchildren to bed, a grandmother took off her makeup, changed into baggy old pants and an oversized t-shirt and washed her hair. In her absence, the children were becoming more and more rambunctious. She shouted at them to keep it down but they just got noisier. Finally, she threw a towel around her head and stormed into their room, saying in a loud voice, "Get right back into bed and I don't want to hear another word!" As she left, she heard the 3-year-old say with a trembling voice, "Who was THAT?"

A second grader came home from school and announced: "We learned how to make babies today."
Her astonished mother said, "Well, that's interesting. So, tell me, how do you make babies?"
"You just change the y to i and add es."

Kids say: keep milk from going sour...keep it in the cow.

A young family moved into a house where another one was being built next door. The five-year-old girl was fascinated by all the activity and hung around,
watching the workers, asking questions, and bringing them glasses of water. They adopted her as a kind of mascot, let her sit with them on their lunch breaks, and gave her little jobs to do here and there. They even gave the child her own hard hat which thrilled her immensely. At the end of a week, they presented her with her "pay envelope" which contained two dollars in dimes. The little girl took her "pay" home and her mother suggested she open a savings account at the bank. Needless to say, the bank teller was charmed. "You must have worked very hard to earn this much," she said. The little girl said, "I worked every day with the guys. We're building a big house." "How interesting. And will you be working next week?"
"It depends," said the little girl,
"whether Home Depot delivers the effing shingles on time."

When my grandson asked me how old I was, I said, "I'm not sure."
"Look in your underwear, grandpa," he advised. "Mine says I'm 4 to 6."

A newly-minted social worker from New York was transferred to a county in Appalachia and was on her first tour of visits, when she came upon the smallest cabin she had ever seen. She knocked on the door and called, "Anybody there?"
"Yep," came a child's voice.
 "How about your Mother?"
 "Ma? Nope, she left just before I got here."
"Is your father there, then?"
 "Nope, he left before Ma came."
"Aren't you ever together as a family?"
"Sure, lady, but not here. This here's the outhouse!"

At pre-school one day, Jenny asked Ari, "Hey, Ari, you wanna play house?"
"Sure," he said. "What do I do?"
The girl said, "I want you to communicate your feelings."
"I don't even know what that means!"
"Perfect," said Jenny.
"You can be the husband."

A young boy comes into the barber shop and the barber whispers to his customer, "This is the world's dumbest kid. Watch this." He puts a dollar bill in one hand and two quarters in the other. Then he calls the boy over and says, "Which one?" The boy takes the two quarters and leaves. "What did I tell you? The kid never learns!"
Later the customer sees the boy on the street and asks, "Tell me, why do you take the two quarters from the barber. You're old enough to know they're worth less."
The boy smiles and says, "Because the day I take the dollar, it's all over!"

KIDS AT SCHOOL

"In wartime children who lived in big cities had to be evaporated because it was safer in the country."

"The total is when you add up all the numbers and a remainder is an animal that pulls Santa on his slay."

"A mosque is a sort of church. The main difference is that its roof is doomed."

"It's wrong to ever split an infinitive."

The Ultimate Bathroom Joke Book

JOKES NOT ABOUT KIDS BUT <u>FOR</u> KIDS

Why did the boy stand on his head?
Because his feet were tired.

Why did the King go to the dentist?
To get his teeth crowned.

How do you prevent a Summer cold?
Catch it in the Winter.

What lies at the bottom of the ocean and twitches?
A nervous wreck.

Why is six scared of seven?
Because 7 8 9.

What kind of car does Luke Skywalker drive?
A Toy-yoda.

When is a car not a car?
When it turns into the garage.

How much do pirates pay for their earrings?
A buccaneer!

What's a myth? A female moth.

Kids in High School were assigned to give a report on two books, "Titanic" and "My Life" by Bill Clinton. Here is one student's report:

Titanic: cost $29.99
Clinton: cost $29.99
***
Titanic: over 3 hours to read
Clinton: over 3 hours to read
***
Titanic: the story of Jack and Rose, their forbidden love and subsequent catastrophe.
Clinton: the story of Bill and Monica, their forbidden love, and subsequent catastrophe.
***
Titanic: Jack teaches Rose to spit.
Clinton: Let's not go there.
***
Titanic: Rose goes down on a vessel full of seamen.
Clinton: Monica...ooh, let's not go there, either.
***
Titanic: Jack surrenders to an icy death.
Clinton: Bill goes home to Hillary: the same thing.

The teacher gave this student an A-plus.

At the end of the school year, Kindergarten kids each gave a gift to the teacher.
When the florist's son handed her a box, she shook it gently and said, "I bet I know what it is. Flowers."
Asked the boy, "How did you know?"
"Just a wild guess," she said.
The next child was the candy shop owner's daughter. The teacher held her gift overhead and said, "I bet I know what it is. A box of candy."
The girl said, "How did you know?"
"Oh, just a wild guess," she said.
The next gift was from the son of the liquor store owner. It was a sizeable box, but it was leaking.
She touched a drop of her tongue, and said: "Is it wine?"
"No," said the boy, smiling broadly.
She put another drop to her tongue and said, "Is it champagne?"
"No, it isn't," said the boy, wriggling with excitement.
The teacher took one more taste before declaring, "I give up. What is it?"
With great glee, the boy cried:
"It's a puppy!"

Little Johnny's neighbors had a new baby, born unfortunately without ears. When Little Johnny's family was invited to visit the new baby, his father explained to him that the baby had no ears. "They'll fix them later," he explained. "But right now, we do not say one single word about no ears, do you understand?" Little Johnny said Yes, he understood.

When little Johnny looked into the crib, he said, "Oh, what a beautiful baby!" The mother said, "Why, thank you." Little Johnny went on. "He has beautiful little feet and beautiful little hands, a cute nose and really beautiful big eyes. Can he see okay?" "Yes," said the mother. "He has perfect vision."

"That's good, because he'd be in big trouble if he needed glasses!"

The math teacher posed the following problem to her class: A wealthy man dies and leaves ten million dollars. One-fifth is to go to his daughter, one-fifth to his son, one-sixth to his brother, and the rest to his wife. Now, what does each one get?

After a very long and puzzled silence, one boy raised his hand and said, "A lawyer?"

DENTIST JOKES KIDS THINK ARE FUNNY

Q: What did the judge say to the dentist?
A: Do you swear to pull the tooth, the whole tooth, and nothing but the tooth?
Q: Has your tooth stopped hurting yet?
A: I don't know. The dentist kept it.
Q: What did the tooth say to the dentist as she left the room?
A: Fill me in when you get back.
Q: Why did the tree go to the dentist?
A: To get a root canal.
Q: What does a dentist get for an award?
A: A little plaque.

A four-year-old girl was learning to say the Lord's Prayer and was saying it all by herself, with no help from her mother.
She recited, "And lead us not into temptation but deliver us some email. Amen."

When I was little, my Dad had me convinced that the ice cream truck only played music when it was sold out.
Well played, Dad, well played.

Who built the ark? I Noah guy.

A college drama group presented a play in which one character would stand on a trap door and announce: "I descend into Hell!" A stagehand below would pull a rope, the trapdoor would open, and the character would plunge through onto a mattress.
The play was well received. When the actor playing that part became ill, another actor—quite overweight—took his place. And when he shouted, "I descend into Hell!" the stagehand pulled the rope, the actor began the plunge; but then became hopelessly stuck. He simply could not descend.
A kind student in the balcony stood up and cried:
"Hallelujah! Hell is full!"

The little boy wasn't getting good marks in school. One day, he surprised his teacher by tapping her on the shoulder. Then he said, "I don't want to scare you, but my Daddy says if I don't get better grades, someone is going to get spanked."

The math teacher called on Little Johnny.
"What are 4, 2, 28 and 44?"
Little Johnny quickly replied: "NBC, CBS, HBO, and the Cartoon Network!"

A father was at the beach with his children when his four-year-old grabbed his hand and led him to the shore, where a seagull lay dead in the sand.
"Daddy, what happened to him?"
"He died and went to heaven," said the father.
The boy thought a moment and then said, "And did God throw him back down?"

After the church service, a little girl told the pastor, "When I grow up, I'm going to give you some money." "Why, thank you," said the pastor. "But, why?"
"Because my Daddy says you're one of the poorest preachers we've ever had."

The teacher showed the class a picture of the Stars and Stripes, and said, "Who can tell me what country has this flag?"
A little girl called out, "That's the flag of <u>our</u> country."
"Very good. And what is the name of our country?"
"Tis of thee," the girl said confidently.

Why did the horse cross the road?
To give the chicken a day off.

A new neighbor asked the little boy if he had brothers and sisters. "No," he said. "I'm the lonely child."

Two brothers were visiting their grandfather, who took them out for lunch. They couldn't make up their minds what they wanted to eat.
With a wink, the grandfather said to the waiter, "Just bring them bread and water." One of the little boys looked up and quavered, "Can I have ketchup on it?"

The teacher of the earth science class was trying to teach map reading. He explained about latitude and longitude, degrees and minutes and asked if there were questions. Blank faces looked up at him. So he said, "Suppose I asked you to meet me for lunch at 23 degrees, 4 minutes north latitude and 45 degrees, 15 minutes east longitude...?" After a confused silence, one girl volunteered, "I guess you'd be eating alone."

What's black and white, black and white, black and white...?
A zebra in a revolving door.

A Sunday school teacher asked, "Who knows the name of Jesus' mother?" "Mary!" "And the name of his father? "Verge."
"Verge? Where do you get that?"
"Well, they're always saying Verge 'n' Mary."

A three-year-old put his shoes on by himself. His mother noticed that the left shoe was on the right foot. She said, "Honey, your shoes are on the wrong feet." He gave her a stare, and said, "Don't try to kid me, Mommy. I <u>know</u> these are my feet."

On the first day of school, the Kindergarten teacher said, "If anyone has to go to the bathroom, hold up two fingers."
A little voice from the back of the room asked, "How will that help?"

Can people predict the future with cards?
My Mom can. Really?
Yes, she takes one look at my report card and tells me what will happen when my Dad gets home.

What do a dog and a baseball player have in common? They both catch flies, chase strays, & run home.

A mother and her young daughter returned from the supermarket and began putting away all the groceries.
The girl opened the box of animal crackers and spread them all over the kitchen table.
"What are you doing?" asked her mother.
"The box says you can't eat them if the seal is broken, and I'm looking for the seal."

CHILDREN'S OPINIONS ABOUT LOVE

"I'm in favor of love as long as it doesn't happen when 'The Simpsons' are on TV."
-Hannah, 6

"Don't do things like have smelly green sneakers. You might get attention but attention ain't the same thing as love."
-Nathan, 9

"I'm not rushing into being in love. I'm finding fourth grade hard enough."
-Ellen, 10

How does a person learn to kiss? "You learn it right on the spot, when the gooshy feelings get the best of you."
–Tony, 7

"One way to get a girl to like you is take her out to eat. Make sure it's something she likes. French fries usually works for me.
-Zach, 9

"It's love if they order one of those desserts that are on fire. They like to order those because it's just like their hearts are on fire."
-Nicole, 9

When is it okay to kiss someone? "It's never okay to kiss a boy. They always slobber all over you...that's why I stopped doing it."
-Pam 10

How to make love endure: "Don't forget your wife's name...that will mess up the love."
-Stephen, 8

"Be a good kisser. It might make your wife forget that you never take the trash out."
-Richard, 8

How do you tell when two people eating in a restaurant are in love? "Just see if the man picks up the check. That's how you can tell if he's in love."
-James, 9

"Love will find you, even if you are trying to hide from it. I've been trying to hide from it since I was five, but the girls keep finding me."
                                                            -Neil, 8

"If you want a girl to fall in love with you, tell her you own a whole bunch of candy stores."
                                                            -Jonah, 6

KID SCIENCE: a fossil is an extinct animal. The older it is, the more extinct it is.

A small boy is put to bed by his father. Five minutes later: "Da...ad!" "What?" "I'm thirsty. Can you bring me a drink of water?" "No, you had your chance. Lights out, buddy."
Five minutes later: "Da...aaaaaad!" "WHAT?" "I'm really thirsty. Please can I have a drink of water?"
"I told you NO. If you ask again, I'll have to spank you!"
Five minutes later: "Da...aaaaaaaaaddy!" "WHAT?!?"
"When you come to spank me, can you please bring me a drink of water?"

An eleven-year-old boy was left in charge of his four-year-old sister while his parents ran an errand. He decided to sit on the riverbank and fish, so he took her along.
"I'll never do <u>that</u> again!" he told his mother that evening. "I didn't catch a single fish!"
"Oh, I'm sure the next time she'll be quiet and not scare the fish away." The boy said, "It wasn't that. She ate all my bait!"

After a particularly stirring church service on Sunday morning, a young boy suddenly announced to his mother, "Mom, I've decided that I want to be a preacher when I grow up."
"That's a fine idea," said his mother, "but what made you decide that?"
"Well," said the boy. "I have to go to church on Sunday and I figure it will be more fun to stand up and yell than to sit and listen."

Little Henry watched, fascinated, as his mother smoothed cold cream on her face.
"Why do you do that, Mommy?"
"To make myself beautiful," she said, and began to remove the cream with a tissue.
"What's the matter, Mommy?" Henry asked. "Are you giving up?"

One day when I was two or three years old, my Grandpa was in charge of me. I had been given a little tea set as a gift and it was one of my favorite toys.
Grandpa was in the living room watching the news when I brought him a little cup of "tea"...just water, of course. He smacked his lips and said it was delicious.
After six or more cups, Grandpa called Grandma in to watch me bring him a cup of tea because it was just the cutest thing. She watched as I went out and came back with a full cup and watched as he drank it down. Then she said, "Has it occurred to you that the only place she can reach to get water is the toilet?"

Debbie Moon's first graders were discussing a picture of a family where just one child was Asian and the rest of the family was not. One girl suggested that the Asian child was adopted. A little girl named Melanie said, "I know all about adoption, because I was adopted."
"What does it mean to be adopted?" asked the teacher.
Said Melanie: "It means that you grew in your Mommy's heart instead of her tummy."

The Sunday School teacher says, "Now, Jeremy tell me the truth. Do you say your prayers before eating?"
"No, ma'am," said Jeremy. "I don't have to. My Mom is a good cook."

That same teacher asks, "Is there a commandment that tells us how to treat our brothers and sisters?" Without missing a beat, a boy says, "Thou shalt not kill."

HOW TO MAKE A MARRIAGE WORK, according to a 10-year-old boy:
"Tell your wife she looks pretty, even if she looks like a truck."

Little Jimmy's preschool class went on a field trip to the local firehouse. The firefighter giving the demonstration held up a smoke detector and asked, "Does anyone know what this is?" Little Jimmy's hand shot up. "That's how Mommy knows supper is ready."

One child answered a question in Social Studies like this: "In Scandinavia, the Danish people come from Denmark, Norwegians come from Norway and the Lapdancers come from Lapland."

This is supposed to be a true story. We all hope so. A little boy in New York City, barefoot and shivering, was staring into one of Macy's windows. A woman approached and said, "Young man, where are your shoes? You shouldn't be barefoot in this weather."
"I was asking God to send me a pair of shoes like the ones in the window," he said.
The woman took the boy into the store, into the children's department, and asked a clerk to please find warm socks and shoes for him; which he quickly did.
After being outfitted with socks and good sneakers, the boy was given an extra pair of socks.
"There you go," said the woman. "I think you'll be much more comfortable now."
The boy looked up at her with tears in his eyes and said, "Are you God's wife?"

Little children have learned that:
No matter how hard you try, you cannot baptize a cat.
When Mom is mad at Dad, don't let her brush your hair.
You can't hide broccoli in your milk.
A turtle will not walk on a leash.

THINGS YOU LEARN FROM YOUR CHILDREN

*Super Glue is forever.

*Always look in the oven before turning it on.

*No matter how much jello you put in the swimming pool, you cannot walk on water.

*Brake fluid mixed with Clorox makes smoke, and lots of it.

*When you hear the toilet flush and the words "Uh-oh," it's already too late.

*If you hook a dog leash over the ceiling fan, the motor is not strong enough to rotate a 42-pound boy wearing Star Wars underwear and a Superman cape.

*The spin cycle on the dryer will not make worms dizzy.

*It will, however, make a cat dizzy.

*Cats throw up twice their body weight when dizzy.

Memorial Day was coming up and the nursery school teacher took the opportunity to talk to her class about patriotism. "We live in a great country," she said. "And the greatest thing about America is that we are all free."
From the back of the room: "I'm not free. I'm four."

IS IT BETTER TO BE MARRIED OR SINGLE?

"You should ask the people who read Cosmopolitan."
-Christy, age 10

"It's better for girls to be single, but not boys. Boys need someone to clean up after them."
-Annie, age 9

"It gives me a headache to think about that stuff. I'm just a kid, I don't need that kind of trouble."
-Will, age 7

"Once I'm done with Kindergarten, I'm going to find me a wife."
-Eric, age 5

LITTLE KIDS' INSTRUCTIONS ON LIFE

"Never trust a dog to watch your food."
—Joy, age 10

"Stay away from prunes."
—Xander, age 9

"Beware of cafeteria food when it looks like it's moving."
—Rob, age 10

"Never do pranks at a police station."
—Sam, age 10

"Remember, you're never too old to hold your father's hand."
—Molly, age 11

"Never tell your Mom her diet's not working."
—Ari, age 14

"Listen to your brain. It has lots of information."
—Chelsea, age 7

"When your Dad is mad and asks, 'Do I look stupid?' don't answer him." —Anna, age 15

When you want something expensive, ask your grandparents.

-Lamar, age 12

ANSWERS GIVEN BY 11-YEAR-OLDS ON SCIENCE EXAMS

The pistol of a flower is the only protection against insects.

A fossil is an extinct animal. The older it is, the more extinct it is.

Liter: a nest of young puppies.

Magnet: something you find crawling over a dead cat.

The skeleton is what is left after the insides have been taken out and the outsides have been taken off.

The purpose of the skeleton is something to hitch meat to.

To prevent contraception, wear a condominium.

For a nosebleed, put the nose much lower than the body until the heart stops.

To remove dust from the eye, pull the eye down over the nose.

A nine-year-old boy surprised his visiting Nana one morning by bringing her a cup of coffee. He proudly announced that he had made it himself. His Nana tasted the coffee—it was awful—and bravely took several sips. She then saw that there were three little metal soldiers in camo gear at the bottom of the cup.
"Honey, what are these Army guys doing in my coffee cup?" she asked.
Her grandson answered: "You know, Nana, it's like on TV. The best part of waking up is soldiers in your cup."

A lady was picking through the frozen turkeys at the grocery store but couldn't find one she considered big enough for her family. She called over a stock boy and said, "Do these turkeys get any bigger?" "No, ma'am," he said. "They're dead."

A 3-year-old prays: Our Father who does art in heaven, Harold is his name. Amen.

A slightly older child says: Lord, if you can't make me a better boy, don't worry about it. I'm having a real good time like I am.

After the christening of his baby brother in church, Jason sobbed all the way home in the back seat of the car. His father asked him three times what was wrong. Finally, Jason said, "The minister said he wanted us brought up in a Christian home, and I want to stay with you guys."

A mother was preparing pancakes for her sons, Roger, 7, and Joe, 3.
The boys began to argue over who would get the first pancake.
Their mother saw an opportunity for a moral lesson.
"If Jesus were sitting here, he would say, 'Let my brother have the first pancake. I can wait.'"
Roger turned to his younger brother and said,
"Joe, you be Jesus."

When I was in my late twenties, I worked as a Kindergarten teacher. One day, while talking to my class seated on the floor around me, I absentmindedly took off my glasses to clean them.
"Wow!" one child exclaimed. "You look really different without your glasses on!"
Another child piped up, "I bet she looks different when she takes her teeth out, too."

The man next door was elderly and had just lost his wife. Upon seeing the man cry, the four-year-old neighbor climbed onto his lap and just sat there.
When his mother asked him what he had said to the old gentleman, the boy said, "Nothing. I just helped him cry."

The summer band class was just getting underway when a large insect flew into the room. The sixth-graders, eager to try their shiny new instruments, tried to ignore the buzzing intruder. Eventually, Eric the tuba player couldn't take the noise. He rolled up his music and swatted the insect, then stomped on it for make sure it was dead.
"Was it a bee?" someone asked.
"Nope," Eric replied. "Bee flat."

KIDS TALK ABOUT LOVE AND MARRIAGE

Q: What would you do on a first date if it wasn't going well?
A: I'd run home and play dead. The next day I'd call all the newspapers and make sure they wrote about me in all the dead columns. -Steven, age 9

Q: What do most people do on a date?
A: Dates are for having fun, and people should use them to get to know each other. Even boys have something to say if you listen long enough.
 -Lynn, age 8
A: On the first date, they just tell each other lies and that gets them interested enough to go for a second date.
 -Bobby, age 10

Q: What's the right age to get married?
A: Twenty-three is the best age because you know the person FOREVER by then.
 -Pam, age 10

A: No age is good to get married at. You got to be a fool to get married at all.
 -Tom, age 7

My mother came by to show off her brand-new Pontiac Grand Am.
My eight-year-old daughter took a look at the car and indignantly proclaimed, "They spelled Grandma wrong!"

My kids' Disney website password is "MickyMinniePlutoGoofy." Why so long? "They said it has to have four characters."

A child wrote: Helicopters are cleverer than planes. Not only can they fly though the air they can also hoover."

Another child: "Then Joan of Ark met her end in a terrible way.
"She was burned as a steak."

A fifth-grade girl asked her mother, "How did I get here?"
Her mother said, "God sent you."
"Did God send you and Daddy, too?"
"Yes, he did."
"Grandma and Grandpa? And their parents?"
"That's right."
"So you're telling me there's been no sex in this family for over 100 years?
"No wonder everyone's so grouchy"

KIDS DISCUSS WHAT LOVE IS

When my grandmother got arthritis, she couldn't bend over and paint her toenails any more. So my grandfather does it for her all the time, even when his hands got arthritis. That's love.
-Becca, age 8

When someone loves you, the way they say your name is different. You know that your name is safe in their mouth.
–Billy, age 4

Love is when a girl puts on perfume and a boy puts on shaving cologne and they go out and smell each other.
-Carrie, age 6

Love is when my Mommy makes coffee for my Daddy and she takes a sip before giving it to him, to make sure the taste is okay.
-Dan, age 7

Love is what's in the room with you at Christmas if you stop opening presents and listen.
-Ethan, age 7

Love is what makes you smile when you're tired.
 -Deborah, age 4

Love is when you tell a guy you like his shirt and then he wears it every day.
 –Marie, 7

Love is like a little old woman and a little old man who are still friends even after they know each other so well.
 –Jerry, age 6

My Mommy loves me more than anybody. You don't see anyone else kissing me to sleep at night.
 -Claire, age 6

Love is when Mommy gives Daddy the best piece of chicken.
 -Noelle, age 5

Love is when Mommy sees Daddy smelly and sweaty and still says he is handsomer than Robert Redford.
–Chris, age 7

During my piano recital, I was on a stage and I was scared. I looked at all the people watching me and saw my Daddy waving and smiling. He was the only one doing that and I wasn't scared any more.
-Cindy, age 8

Love is when your puppy licks your face even after you left him alone all day.
Mary Ann, age 7

While waiting with his mother in the doctor's office, a four year old walked over to a pregnant woman.
"Why is your stomach so big?" he asked.
She replied: "I'm having a baby."
With big eyes, he asked, "Is the baby in your stomach?"
"He sure is."
The little boy looked quite puzzled. "Is it a bad baby?"
She said, "Oh, no, he is a real good baby."
With an even more surprised look, he asked, "Then why did you eat him?"

Kid's advice: Never do pranks at a Police Station.

Other kid's advice: Stay away from prunes.
A 9-year-old girl's take on marriage:
When somebody's been dating for a while, the boy might propose to the girl. He says to her, "I'll take you for a whole life, or at least until we have kids and get divorced. But you got to do one particular thing for me." Then she says yes, but she's wondering what the thing is and whether it's naughty or not. She can't wait to find out.

YOUNGSTERS' VIEWS ON LIFE
Beware of cafeteria food when it looks like it's moving.
-Rob, age 10

Never tell your little brother that you're not going to do what you mom told you to do.
-Hank, age 12

When you get a bad grade in school, show it to your Mom when she's on the phone.
-Ayesha, age 13

Don't flush the john when your Dad's in the shower.
-Lamar, age 10

Never ask for anything that costs more than five dollars when your parents are doing their taxes.

-Carol, age 9

Don't pick on your sister when she's holding a baseball bat.

-Joe, age 12

Sleep in your clothes so you'll be dressed in the morning.

-Stephanie, age 8

Wear a hat when feeding seagulls. –Bill, 9

KIDS TALK ABOUT MARRIAGE

Marriage is when you get to keep your girl and don't have to give her back to her parents.

-Eric, age 6

You flip a nickel and heads means you stay with him and tails means you try the next one.

-Kelly, age 9

I can't think about that. It gives me a headache. I'm just a kid.

–John, age 8

You should never kiss a girl unless you have enough bucks to buy her a ring and her own VCR 'cause she'll want to have videos of the wedding.

-Andy, age 10

My Mom and Dad met at a dance party at a friend's house. Then they went for a drive, but the car broke down. It was a good thing, because it gave them a chance to find out about their values.

-Debbie, age 9

You should be 84 before you get married because at that age, you don't have to work anymore, and you can spend all your time loving each other in your bedroom.

-Pam, 8

A very dirty little boy came in from playing in the yard and asked his mother,
 "Who am I?"
Ready to play the game, she said, "I don't know. Who are you?"
"Wow!" cried the child. "Mrs. Gallo was right! She said I was so dirty, my own mother wouldn't recognize me!"

Here's how 11-year-old kids see science:

A permanent set of teeth consists of eight canines, eight cuspids, two molars, and eight cuspidors.

Germinate: to become a German.

The tides are a fight between the Earth and Moon. All water tends towards the moon, because there is no water in the moon, and nature abhors a vacuum.
I forget where the sun joins in this fight.

For head cold, use an agonizer to spray the nose until it stops in your throat.

For dog bite, put the dog away for several days. If he has not recovered, then kill it.

For asphyxiation: apply artificial respiration until the patient is dead.

For fainting, rub the person's chest or, if a lady, rub her arm above the wrist. .

A planet is a large body of earth surrounded by sky.

When my friend Phyllis found out she was pregnant, she lit up the internet and phone lines, telling everyone the good news.
One day the following week, she and her four-year-old, Sam, were out shopping and bumped into an old friend.
The friend asked Sam if he was excited about the baby.
"Yes," he said proudly, "and I know what we're going to name it. If it's a girl, we're calling her Molly and if it's a boy, we're going to call it quits."

Two kids share a room in the hospital.
The first kid says, "What are you here for?"
The second kid says, "I'm here to get my tonsils out and I'm really a little nervous."
The first kid said,
"Oh, yeah, I had that once. They put you to sleep and when you wake up, they give you lots of jello and ice cream. It's not bad!"
The second kid said, "Yeah, that sounds pretty okay. What are you in for?"
"I'm here for a circumcision."
"Whoa!" said the other kid.
"I had that done when I was born.
"I couldn't walk for a whole year!"

CHILDISH MISUNDERSTANDINGS

A mosque is a sort of church. The main difference is that its roof is doomed.

I asked my mom why we said old men at the end of prayers at school, I don't know any old men apart from grandpa.

Sometimes in the war they take prisners and keep them as ostreiges until the war is over. Some prisners end up in consterpation camps.

...and at the end of the show we all sing away in a manager.

In last year's Christmas concert, Linzi played the main prat. I played one of the smaller prats and I would like to have a bigger prat this year.

Sir Walter Raleigh circumcised the world with a big clipper.

The total is when you add up all the numbers and a remainder is an animal that pulls santa on his slay.

In wartime children who lived in big cities had to be evaporated because it was safer in the country.

If it is less than 90 degrees it is a cute angel.

The closet town to France is Dover. You can get to France on a train or you can go on a fairy.

In geography we learned that countries with sea round them are islands and ones without sea are incontinents.

Crabs and creatures like them all belong to a family of crushed asians.

If you marry two people you are a pigamist but morons are allowed to do this.

I'd like to be an accountant, but they have to know a lot about moths.

TEACHER: Jake, why are you doing your multiplication work on the floor?
JAKE: You said to do it without tables.

Two small boys, not yet old enough to be in school, were overheard talking at the playground one day.
"My name is Billy," said one. "What's yours?"
"My name is Kyle," said the second boy.
"My Daddy's a teacher in college. What does your Daddy do?"
Billy said, "My Daddy is a lawyer."
"Honest?" asked Kyle.
"No, just the regular kind."

A school psychologist was asked to talk with a boy who draws all his pictures with only black or brown crayons.
She chats with the boy. He seems fine, a bit shy but cheerful and ready to answer questions.
She gives him projective tests and nothing shows up.
Finally, kind of desperate, she gives him some paper and a box of crayons.
"Oh, goody!" exclaims the boy. "In school, I get an old box all the time with only brown and black."

A child's eagerness to assist in a project varies in inverse proportion to his ability.

Put two kids in a roomful of toys, and it's certain that both of them will want to play with the same one.

One of life's greatest mysteries is how the boy who wasn't good enough for your daughter can be the father of the smartest, cutest grandchild in the world.

Warning on the kid's toy, Magic 8 Ball: Not advised for use as a pregnancy test.

The teacher is giving his class a quiz. The last question was "What are the last two lines of *The Star-Spangled Banner?*
One bright youngster wrote: "And the home of the brave, play ball."

A seven year old is talking to his friend who is six. "I found a condom on the patio," says the seven year old. Says the six year old: "What's a patio?"

A teenager says to the doctor, "My friend has a problem. He thinks he might have VD. What should he do?"
Doctor: "Take out your friend, and let's have a look at him."

The first grade teacher was reading the story of Chicken Little to her class. She got to the part where Chicken Little tells the famer, "The sky is falling! The sky is falling!" The teacher asked, "And what do you think the farmer said?"
A little girl called out, "Oh my God, a talking chicken!!"

The neighbor noticed little Tim busy digging a hole on his side of the fence. "What're you doing there, Tim?" he asked. "Burying my goldfish," said a tearful Tim. "That's a pretty big hole for a goldfish," said the neighbor. Tim said, "That's because he's inside your murdering cat!"

A Kindergarten child told his teacher he had found a dead cat. She asked him how he knew the cat was dead. "Because I pissed in his ear," said the child. "You did WHAT?" cried the teacher. "I leaned over and said "Pssst!" in his ear and he didn't move."

A 3-year-old noticed his private parts while in the bathtub. "Are these my brains?" he asked.
Said his mother: "Not yet."

The Ultimate Bathroom Joke Book

THIS AND THAT

A Jewish grandma takes her grandson to the beach. He's playing in the water, she's standing on the shore. Suddenly a huge wave breaks directly over the spot where the boy is playing. The water recedes and the boy is gone.

The grandmother lifts her arms to the heavens, sobbing and weeping.

"Lord, God, how could you do this to me? Haven't I been a wonderful mother and grandmother? Haven't I kept a kosher home, given to charity, lit candles every Friday night?

"How could you take from me my beloved Danny, my beloved only grandson, who never did a wrong thing in his life? Please, God, listen to me and hear my voice!"

From the sky, a voice booms, "All right! All right already! Stop!"

A moment later, another wave appears and when the water recedes, the little boy is there, smiling and splashing as if nothing happened.

The voice booms: "I have answered your prayers and returned to you your grandson. Are you satisfied now?"

She says: "He had a hat."

The sole purpose of a child's middle name is so he can tell when he's really in trouble.

My father thinks I should marry a girl who has the same belief as my family. I say to him, "Dad, why would I marry a girl who thinks I'm a loser?"

FROM AN ARAB STUDENT TO HIS FATHER:
Dear Father, New York is wonderful, people are nice and I really like it here. But Dad, I'm a bit ashamed to arrive at NYU with my pure gold Ferrari 599GTB when all my teachers and many fellow students travel by train. Your son, Nasser
ANSWER FROM HIS FATHER TO NASSER:
My dear son, Twenty million USD has just been transferred to your account. Please stop embarrassing us.
Go and get yourself a train, too.

A blonde goes to work, crying her eyes out. "My Mom died," she explains and the boss offers her the day off. But she wants to keep busy. Later that day, she's weeping again. "More bad news?" he asks.
"My sister just called and said her Mom died, too!"

It's a little known story but the Goldberg brothers, Lowell, Norman, Hiram and Max, invented and brought their auto air conditioner into Henry Ford's office on July 17,1946, when the temperature in Detroit was 97 degrees. Henry Ford was well known as an anti-Semite and the only way they got in was through his secretary, a Jewish girl who was passing for gentile.

She told Mr. Ford that four gentlemen had brought in an invention that was the best thing since the electric starter. They wanted to show him how their invention worked in their car. Intrigued, Mr. Ford was persuaded to get into the car which by then was about 130 degrees. One of them turned on the a/c and the car quickly cooled off. Mr. Ford instantly offered them 3 million for the patent. The brothers said they would take two million, on condition there was a label "The Goldberg Air-Conditioner" on the dashboard of every Ford car. Ford refused. No way was a Jewish name appearing in every Ford car! Back and forth they went, finally agreeing to 4 million and just their first names would be used. And so it is to this day: all Ford air-conditioners say Lo, Norm, Hi, and Max on the controls.

A friend told the blonde, "Christmas is on a Friday this year."
The blonde said, "Let's hope it's not the 13th."

Woman's t-shirt slogan: And your point is...

A blonde goes to the vet with her goldfish.
"I think it's got epilepsy," she says.
The vet takes a look and says, "The fish seems calm enough to me."
She says, "I haven't taken it out of the bowl yet."

Flight Attendant: Would you like dinner?
Passenger: What are my choices?
Flight Attendant: Yes or no.

The police officer got out of his car as the kid who was stopped for speeding rolled down his window.

"I've been waiting for you all day," the cop said.

The kid replied: "Well, I got here as fast as I could."

When the cop finally stopped laughing, he sent the kid on his way without a ticket.

A guy is driving around the backwoods of Montana and sees a hand-written sign tacked to the door of a small log cabin. TALKING DOG FOR SALE.
The owner appears and tells him the dog is tied up in the back yard. The guy goes into the back yard where he sees a nice looking Labrador retriever sitting in the shade. "You talk?" "Yep," says the lab. The guy almost can't believe his ears. "So what's your story?" he asks. "Well," says the dog. "I discovered I could talk when I was quite young so I went to the nearest Army recruiting station and asked what I could do. In no time, I was jetting around the world with the CIA and sitting in on secret enemy meetings because, hey, I'm only a dog, right? Who would suspect me? But, let me tell you, the work of a spy is no picnic. After five years, I got out, got myself a wife, had a mess of puppies and now I'm just retired." Wow! The guy thinks. He runs back and asks "How much for the dog?"
"Ten bucks."
"$10? But that dog really talks!"
"Yeah, but he's a liar. He's never been out of the yard."

I'm over the hill, but the climb was great!

I once wanted to become an atheist, but I gave up. They have no holidays.
-Henny Youngman

The remarkable thing about my mother is that for 30 years she served us nothing but leftovers. The original meal has never been found.
–Calvin Trillin

Humility is no substitute for a good personality.
-Fran Lebowitz

My idea of an agreeable person is someone who agrees with me.
-Benjamin Disraeli

It's so simple to be wise. Just think of something stupid to say and don't say it.
-Sam Levenson

I went on a diet, swore off drinking and heavy eating and in 14 days I had lost exactly two weeks.
-Joe E. Lewis

I have enough money to last me the rest of my life unless I buy something.
-Jackie Mason

I once was indecisive. Now I'm not so sure.
—Steven Wright

Television is a medium because it is neither rare nor well done.
-Ernie Kovaks

A blonde woman was speeding down the road in her little red sports car and was pulled over by a woman police officer, also blonde. The blonde cop asked to see her driver's license, registration and insurance. The driver dug and dug through her handbag, getting more and more agitated. Finally, she said, "What does my driver's license look like?"
"It's square and it has your picture on it."
The driver went through her purse some more and came up with a small mirror, looked at it, and handed it to the policewoman. "Here it is," she said.
The blonde policewoman looked at the mirror, then handed it back. "OK, you can go. I didn't realize you were a cop."

The Red Cross just asked if we could contribute to the floods in Pakistan. We'd like to but our garden hose only reaches the driveway.

A truck driver doesn't notice the Low Bridge Ahead sign and, sure enough, his truck is wedged under the bridge. Cars are backed up for miles.
Finally, a police car arrives. The cop looks, hands on hips, and says, "Got stuck, huh?"
"No," says the driver. "I was delivering this bridge when I ran out of gas."

You take a bat, a ball, a glove. What've you got? America's favorite pastime: shopping.

A man and his wife took a vacation by driving across the country in their RV. At one point, they were nearing a town called KISSAMEE; and they spent some time discussing how in the world it might be pronounced. KISS-a-me? Ki-SAM-me? Kissa-MEE?
Pretty soon they reached the town and pulled into a place to get something to eat. The man said to the girl behind the counter, "My wife and I can't seem to be able to figure out how to pronounce the name of this place. Would you mind telling me where we are? Say it very slowly so that I can remember it, please." The girl stared at him and droned: "Buuuurger Kiiinnng."

This woman was having a passionate affair with the inspector from a pest control company. One afternoon, they were carrying on in the bedroom when unexpectedly her husband came home. She pushed her naked lover into the closet and sweetly said hello to her husband. He was a suspicious man and soon discovered the man in the closet.
"Who are you?" "An inspector from Bugs Begone."
"You're in my closet, why?"
"I'm investigating a complaint about an infestation of moths."
"With no clothes on?"
The inspector looked down at himself and exclaimed, "Those little bastards!"

I was standing in a bar and this little Chinese guy comes in and stands next to me. I said to him, "Do you know any of those martial arts things, like kung-fu or tae quan do or ju jitsu?" "Why do you ask me such a question," he demanded. "Is it because I'm Asian?"

"No," I said. "It's because you're drinking my effing beer."

Outside of a dog, a book is your best friend. Inside of a dog, it's too dark to read.

What are 3 words a woman never wants to hear when she's making love?
"Honey, I'm home!"

Before you diagnose yourself with depression, first make sure you are not, in fact, surrounded by assholes.

Father O'Brien answers the phone.
"Hello, is this Father O'Brien?"
"It is."
"This is the IRS. Can you help us?"
"I can."
"Do you know a Pat Connery?"
"I do."
"Is he a member of your congregation?"
"He is."
"Did he donate $10,000 to the church?"
"He will!"

The new sultan goes into his harem, where women of all ages and sizes wait for him. He says, "I know what I'm supposed to do but I'm not sure where to begin."

A psychiatrist tells his most difficult case. "This patient lived in a fantasy world. He believed an uncle in Florida was going to die and leave him a fortune. He never went out, in case the letter came. I worked with him for seven years and finally, I cured him. And then that damn letter arrived!"

The man came rushing into the dentist's office. "Listen, I'm in a hurry. I have two buddies sitting in my truck, waiting for us to go deer hunting, so forget about any fancy anesthetic. Just pull the tooth and we'll be on our way!"
The dentist was impressed. "You don't want anything to kill the pain? Nothing?"
"Nothing! Come on! I'm really in a hurry!"
So the dentist said, "Which tooth is it?"
The man turned to his wife and said, "Open your mouth, Honey, and show him."

The scene is on the ocean at night.
The ship's captain sees a light ahead. He sends a message: "This is an order, divert your course 10 degrees. I am the captain of a battleship."
The return message: "You had better divert 10 degrees. I am a light house."

ETERNAL QUESTIONS

\# Why do people say they "slept like a baby" when babies wake up every couple of hours?

\# How come we put a man on the moon BEFORE we figured out that wheels on luggage was a good idea?

\# Why do doctors leave the room while you change, since they're going to see you naked anyway?

\# Why doesn't Tarzan have a beard?

\# If a deaf person goes to court, is it still a "hearing

\#How many roads must a man travel down before he admits that he's lost?

Mary Clancy goes up to Father O'Leary after the ten o'clock Mass and she's in tears. "What in the world is bothering you, Mary?" She says, "Oh Father, I have terrible news! My husband Danny passed away last night!"
"Oh, Mary, that's terrible," says the priest. "Did he have any last requests?"
"That he did, Father.
"He said, 'Please, Mary, put down that gun.'"

A woman goes to a psychiatrist. He gives her a tranquilizer. After a week, he asks, "How are you?" She says, "Who cares?"

A man goes into a bar and orders seven whisky shots, doubles. The bartender watches in wonder as the guy drinks one after the other without a pause.
"Why are you drinking so hard?" he asks.
"You'd drink like this if you had what I have," says the customer.
"And what's that?"
"One dollar."

A drunk was weaving down the alley carrying a box with holes in the sides. He bumped into a friend, who said, "What do you have in there?" He replied: "A mongoose."
"A mongoose? Why?"
"You know how drunk I get and then I see snakes."
"But those snakes are imaginary!"
"That's okay. So is the mongoose."

The difference between a lady and a diplomat. When a lady says No, she means Maybe. When she says Maybe, she means Yes. If she says Yes, she's no lady.
When a diplomat says Yes, he means Maybe. When he says Maybe, he means No. And if he says No, he's no diplomat.

A BIT OF JOAN RIVERS

I hate housework. You make the beds, you wash the dishes and 6 months later, you have to start all over again.

I succeeded by saying what everyone else was thinking.

Was Elizabeth Taylor fat? Her favorite food was seconds.

I wish I had a twin so I could see what I'd look like without plastic surgery.

If God wanted us to bend over, He'd put diamonds on the floor.

I told my mother-in-law that my house was her house and she said "Get the hell off my property!"

My vagina is like Newark. Everyone knows where it is but nobody goes there anymore.

I met my husband at the door wrapped in Saran.
He said, "What, leftovers again?"

THINGS THAT MAYBE YOU DIDN'T KNOW

Ships and airplanes use "Mayday" as their SOS.
It's because the French for "Help!" Is "M'aidez"
Pronounced—you guessed it--"mayday."

In tennis the score of zero is called love. Here come the French again. Since a zero on the scoreboard looked like an egg, they called it "l'ouef" which is French for egg. Then when tennis came to America, we mispronounced it as "love."

We clink our glasses together before drinking a toast and there are people who get upset if they don't get "clinked." It all began when enemies were often killed by poisoned drink; so a host would pour a small amount from his glass into other glasses and all drank. When a guest trusted his host, he would only touch the other's glass... and now we all do it.

When someone is happy, we say he is "on Cloud Nine." Clouds are numbered according to the altitudes they reach and 9 is highest.

A Jewish couple in London won 20 million pounds in the lottery. They bought themselves a magnificent mansion and all the trappings that go with it, including a very proper, very British butler.
The day after his arrival, he was instructed to set up the dining table for four, as they had invited the Levys for luncheon. Then they left the house to do some shopping. When they returned, they found the table set for six. Perplexed, they asked the butler why he had not set up as they had asked. The butler explained, "The Levys called and said they were bringing the Blintzes."

The local news station was interviewing an 80-year-old woman who had just married for the fourth time.
"He's a funeral director," she said. This naturally led into a discussion about her first three husbands and what they did for a living .She explained that her first husband was a banker; her second a circus ringmaster; and the third, a preacher. Why such diversity, asked the interviewer. She smiled and said:
"One for the money, two for the show, three to get ready...and four, to go."

PET PEEVES DOGS HAVE ABOUT HUMANS

1) Yelling at me for barking. Hey! I'm a DOG!

2) Taking me out for a walk, then not letting me check stuff out.
Exactly whose walk IS this, anyway?

3) Any trick that involves balancing food on my nose...
Stop it!

4) Any haircut that involves bows or ribbons.
Now you know why we chew your stuff up when you're not home.

5) That sleight of hand fake-fetch throw. You fooled a dog! Whoo-hoo!! What a proud moment for the top of the food chain.

6) Sorry about sniffing crotches...I haven't got the hang of shaking hands yet.

7) Dog sweaters. Hello?? Haven't you noticed the fur?

PEOPLE FROM THE SOUTH ARE JUST DIFFERENT

Favorite Southerners' swimmin' spots:
The beach...the rivuh...the crick.

Southerners know everyone's name:
Honey ... darlin' ... shugah.

Prevalent Southern religions:
Bapdiss ... Methdiss ... football.

Southern cities just drippin' with charm:
Chawl'stn ... S'vanah ... Foat Wuth ... N'awlins

Southern elegant gentlemen:
Men in uniform ... men in tuxedos ... Rhett Butler

Only a Southerner knows how many fish, collard greens, turnip greens, peas, beans and rice make up a "mess."

Only a Southerner both knows and understands the difference between a redneck, a good ol' boy, and po' white trash.

Southerners know how to cook and eat grits.

Put 100 Southerners in a room and half of them will discover they're related, even if only by marriage.

Only true Southerners say "sweet tea" and "sweet milk." Sweet tea indicates the need for sugar and lots of it. Sweet milk means not buttermilk.

When you hear someone say, "Well, I caught myself lookin'," you know you are in the presence of a genuine Southerner.

All true Southerners know you don't scream obscenities at little old ladies who drive 30 mph in the left lane on the highway. You just say, "Why, bless her sweet little heart," and pass her on the right.

Southerners say they're fixin' to do somethin' or othah.

To those of you who are still having a hard time understanding all this Southern stuff... Why, bless your hearts, I hear they're fixin' to have classes in Southern as a second language.
See all y'all there!

BUREAUCRACIES NEVER DIE

The U.S. standard railroad has a distance between the rails of four feet, 8.5 inches. That's really odd spacing. Why was that gauge used? Because that's how they built them in England and English expatriates designed the U.S. railroads. But how come the English built them like that? Because the first rail lines were built by the same folks who built the tramways and that's the gauge they used. And why was that the gauge used for the tramways? Because the people who built the tramways used the same jigs and tools they already had for building wagons, which used that wheel spacing. Again, why? Because the old long-distance roads in England had deep ruts which were four feet, 8.5 inches apart and the wagon wheels had to fit. Imperial Rome built all the long-distance roads in England and much of Europe. Roman war chariot wheels were four feet, 8.5 inches apart and everyone who came after had to build to those specifications or their wheels would break. So the U.S. standard rail gauge is derived from specs for a Roman war chariot. Bureaucracies never die.

AND THEN THE FIGHT STARTED

My wife sat down on the couch next to me as I was flipping through the channels and asked, "What's on TV?" "Dust," I answered.
And then the fight started.

My wife was hinting about what she'd like for our anniversary. "I'd love something shiny and sleek that goes from 0 to 150 in about 3 seconds." I bought her a scale.
And then the fight started.

When I got home last night, my wife asked to be taken somewhere expensive. So, I took her to a gas station.
And then the fight started.

I rear-ended a car this morning. We both pulled over and the other driver got out. I was surprised to see that he was a little person, a dwarf.
He stormed over to my car, looked up at me, and said sternly, "I am not happy!"
I looked down at him and said, "Well, then, which one are you?"
And then the fight started.

A wise man said once, and only once: "I don't know ... ask a woman."

Noticing a sign on the main street saying "Fortune Teller Upstairs" a woman decided to give it a try.
In a darkened room, the mystic peered into her crystal ball, then looked up and said, "There's no easy way for me to tell you this. Your husband will die a violent death within the year!"
Visibly shaken, the woman took in a deep breath. Then she met the fortune teller's gaze and said, "Will I be acquitted?"

Three blond men are stranded on one side of a wide river and don't know how to get to the other side. A genie appears and says each man can have a wish. The first man wishes that he'll be smart enough to figure out a way to get across. Poof! He realizes he can swim across. The second blond wants to be smarter and not have to work so hard. Poof! A boat appears and he rows across easily. The third blond guy asks the genie to make him the smartest of all.
Poof! He's turned into a woman and walks across the bridge.

The Ultimate Bathroom Joke Book

SLOGANS FOR WOMEN'S TEE'S

I'm out of estrogen. But I have a gun.

All stressed out and no one to choke.

Of course I don't look busy.
I did it right the first time.

I'm one of those bad things
that happen to good people

You have the right to remain silent,
so please SHUT UP!

I'm busy. You're ugly. Have a nice day.

Guys have feelings, too.
But, like, who cares?

I don't believe in miracles. I rely on them.

Warning! Next mood swing: 6 minutes.

I used to be schizophrenic,
but we're okay now.

I can talk and annoy you all at once.

A tough guy walks into a bar and is about to order a drink when he sees a man close by with long locks of hair in front of his ears and wearing a kippa on his head. He doesn't have to be an Einstein to see that this guy is Jewish. The tough guy doesn't like Jews.
So he shouts loudly to the bartender: "Drinks for everyone in the house...except the Jew."
Soon after the drinks have been handed out, the Jewish fellow gives him a wave and says loudly, "Thank you!"
What's going on? The tough guy is infuriated. Once again, he loudly orders drinks for the house...but not for the Jew.
As before, the Jewish man continues to smile and say, "Thank you!"
The tough guy says to the bartender, "What the hell is wrong with that Jew? I've ordered two rounds for everyone but him, and all he does is smile and thank me. What's with him? Is he nuts?"
"No," says the bartender. "He owns the place."

WARNING: the consumption of alcohol may cause you to tell the same boring story over and over and over and over.

The man spoke frantically into the phone: "My wife is pregnant and her contractions are only two minutes apart!"
"Is this her first child?" the doctor asked.
"No!" the man shouted. "This is her husband!"

Long ago in Texas, a Mexican came across the border and robbed a bank. They caught him quickly, but there was no money on him. Where was the money hidden?
The thief spoke no English so the sheriff called for an interpreter.
"Ask him if he admits robbing the bank."
Yes, the interpreter told him.
The sheriff cocked his pistol and held it to the thief's head. "Ask him where he hid the money."
The bandit told the interpreter that he threw the money down the town well.
"He says he is not afraid to die."

You're only young once. After that, you need a new excuse.

I prefer the term homemaker because housewife implies there's another wife somewhere.
-Bella Abzug

Mother One: My son is a judge and when he walks into a room, they call him Your Honor.
Mother Two: My son is a bishop and when people see him come in, they call him Excellency.
Mother Three: My son is a cardinal and when he enters, the people call him Your Eminence.
Mother Four: Well, my son is Shaquille O'Neill and when people see him coming, they say, "Oh, my God!"

A man at a bar spotted a young woman so gorgeous he couldn't stop staring at her. Of course, she noticed and came over to him. Before he could apologize for his rudeness, she said, "I'll do anything, absolutely anything you want, no matter how kinky, for $100. But there's one condition."
The startled man asked what the condition was.
She said, "You have to tell me what you want me to do in just three words."
The man thought for a minute, then took out his wallet and counted out five $20 bills.
He pressed the money into her hand, looked deep into her eyes, and very clearly said, "Paint my house."

10 THINGS ONLY WOMEN UNDERSTAND

10. Why it's necessary to have 6 pairs of black shoes.

9. The difference between, ivory, off-white, and cream.

8. Crying can be fun.

7. FAT CLOTHES

6. Salad, diet soda and chocolate are a balanced meal.

5. Discovering a designer dress that fits on the clearance rack is a peak experience.

4. Every scale ever made is inaccurate, period.

3. A good man might be hard to find, but a good hairdresser? Almost impossible.

2. Why a phone call with a girlfriend never lasts less than 10 minutes.

1. OTHER WOMEN!

Why will someone believe you when you say there are 4 billion stars, but check when you say the paint is wet?

A man went to the toy store to buy his daughter the birthday present she really wanted: a Barbie Doll. He had no idea there were so many different Barbies! So he asked a clerk for help. "Which one should I get?"
"Well, I can show you the most popular ones. Here we have Malibu Barbie with bathing suit and towel, for $12. Here's the Ballerina Barbie for $22, which comes with tutu and cassette. We have Aerobics Barbie for $20 which includes a leotard and workout DVD. And, oh, here's the newest one: Divorce Barbie, for $1200.
The man was flabbergasted. "Why is this one so much more than the others?"
"Simple," replied the clerk. "Divorce Barbie comes with Ken's car, Ken's boat, Ken's house..."

My mother said, "Judy, you'll never amount to anything because you procrastinate."
I said, "Yeah? Just wait!"
                                        –Judy Tenuta

As soon as she had finished Parochial School, a talented girl named Sally shook the dust of Duluth off her feet and headed for New York, where she became a successful performer in show business. Eventually, she returned to her home town and on a Saturday night, went to confession in the church she had attended as a child. In the confessional, the priest recognized her and asked about her career. She said she would be happy to show him the sort of thing she did on stage, "acrobatic dancing, it's called."
She stepped out of the confessional and went into a series of cartwheels, leaping splits, handsprings and backflips, all done expertly.
Two middle-aged ladies waiting to confess watched her, mouths open. One said to the other, "Oh, my! Just look at the penances Father Sullivan is giving out tonight...and me without my bloomers on!"

"Have you seen Harris lately?"
"Well, I have and I haven't...I saw a guy who I thought was Harris and he saw a fella he thought was me. But when we got closer, it was neither of us."

The Republican Party is changing its symbol from elephant to condom. A condom allows for inflation, halts production, destroys the next generation, protects a bunch of dicks and gives you a sense of security while you're actually being screwed.
It just doesn't get more accurate than that!

If you want someone who is content to get on your bed just to warm your feet and whom you can push off if he snores...then get a dog! If you want someone who will never touch the remote and watch romantic movies with you...get a dog. If you want someone who never criticizes, doesn't care if you are pretty or ugly, young or old, fat or thin, black or white, who acts as if every word you say is special, and loves you unconditionally... then get a dog!
BUT, on the other hand, if you want someone who will never come when you call, totally ignores you when you come home, leaves hair all over the place, walks all over you, runs around all night, only comes home to eat and sleep, and acts as if your whole existence is solely to ensure his happiness... by all means get a cat. You figured I was going to say ... marry a man, didn't you?

We'll start with Imperial Rome for this true story. Roman Army chariots were built just wide enough to accommodate the rear-ends of two war horses.

Now we'll go forward in time to our space shuttles. When you see a shuttle sitting on the launch pad, there are two big booster rockets attached to the sides of the fuel tank. These are Solid Rocket Boosters, or SRBs.

The designers of the SRBs would have preferred to make them a bit wider but the railway line from the factory to the launch site ran through a tunnel in the mountains and they wouldn't fit.

The tunnel is slightly wider than the railroad track which—if you were paying attention a few pages back—has the exact same measurements as the tracks for war chariots in ancient Rome.

So, a major space shuttle design feature of what is probably the world's most advanced transportation system was determined over 2,000 years ago by the width of a horse's behind.

And you thought being a horse's ass wasn't important!

Two blind pilots, both wearing dark glasses, made their way onto a jet airliner. One was using a guide dog and the other a tapping white cane, as they made their way along the aisle. Nervous laughter spread through the cabin as the men entered the cockpit and closed the door. As the engines revved up, the passengers began to glance nervously around, searching for a sign that this was just a little practical joke. But all was as usual in the cabin and the attendants began their usual call to buckle up and look for the exits.

The plane began to taxi down the runway and, as this was LaGuardia Airport in New York, people sitting in the window seats were aware that the plane was headed straight for the water. At first there was nervous silence; then, as the plane did not deviate from its course, hysterical screams filled the cabin.

At that moment, the plane lifted smoothly into the air and the passengers began to relax and laugh a bit sheepishly.

In the cockpit, one of the blind pilots turned to the other and said, "Ya know, Bob, one of these days, they're gonna scream too late and we're all gonna die."

A wrinkled little old lady sold pretzels on a street corner in Chicago for a dollar apiece. Every day a young man would leave his office building at lunch time, and as he passed the pretzel stand, he would leave her a dollar. He never took a pretzel.

This went on for three years. The two of them never spoke. One day as the young man passed the pretzel stand and left his usual offering, the pretzel lady spoke to him for the first time.
"They're a dollar and a quarter now."

The time is at hand when the wearing of a prayer shawl and a skullcap will not bar a man from the White House—unless, of course, the man is Jewish.
–J. Farber

Lenny Bruce said: Even if you are Catholic, if you live in New York, you're Jewish. If you live in Salt Lake City, Utah, you are going to be a goy even if you <u>are</u> Jewish.

Golda Meir said this: Let me tell you something I have against Moses. He took us for forty years into the desert in order to bring us to the one place in the Middle East that has no oil!

As a bagpiper I am asked to play at many funerals, so I was happy to do a gig at the graveside of a homeless man who had nobody to mourn him.
He was buried in a pauper's cemetery in the backwoods of Kentucky so of course I got lost and was an hour late. Nobody was there but the diggers and they were eating lunch. I felt really bad and apologized to them. I looked down into the grave and the vault lid was already in place. I didn't know what else to do so I started to play. The workmen gathered round. I played from the heart for this unknown, homeless man. As I played "Amazing Grace," the workers began to weep. They cried, I cried. It was amazing! When I finished, I packed up and started for my car, my head low but my heart full. As I opened the car door, I heard one of the workers say, "I never seen nothin' like this before and I've been putting in septic tanks for twenty years."

It was Mort Sahl who said: Liberals feel unworthy of their possessions.
Conservatives feel they deserve everything they've stolen.

Here's something you may not know: When Mary Queen of Scots went to France as a very young woman, Louis, King of France, learned that she loved the Scots game of golf. So Louis had the first golf course outside of Scotland built for her enjoyment. To make sure she was properly chaperoned (and guarded) while she played, Louis hired cadets from a military school to accompany her around the course while she played. Mary enjoyed their company and liked having her clubs carried around for her; so when she returned to Scotland (not a very good idea in the long run) she took the idea with her. In French, the word cadet is pronounced ca-DAY and it was soon changed to caddy by the Scots.

Heinrich Heine said: God will pardon me; it's His business.

Ninety-Nine percent of men give the other one percent a bad name.

Why do you need to wear a winter coat to shine the car?
Because the container says you need a heavy coat to make the shine last longer.

Dimes and quarters are notched around the edges, while nickels and pennies are not. Why? Once, dimes and quarters contained silver and people would take shavings to sell. Notching put an end to that. Nickels and pennies, on the other hand, were not made of anything that valuable; so, no notches.

TECHNICAL SUPPORT: Okay, sir, press the control and escape keys at the same time. That will bring up a task list. Now type the letter "P" to get the Program Manager.
CUSTOMER: I don't have a "P."
TECH SUPPORT: On your keyboard, sir. "P"...on your keyboard.
CUSTOMER: I AM NOT GOING TO DO THAT!

A new supermarket opened near our house. It has an automatic water mister in the produce section and before it goes on, you hear the sound of distant thunder and smell fresh rain. Near the milk cases, you hear cows mooing and smell fresh hay. Near the egg section, you hear clucking and cackling and in the air, there is the aroma of eggs and bacon cooking. The produce section features the smell of fresh buttered corn. I don't buy toilet paper there any more!

THOSE ROTTEN WOMEN DRIVERS!

I was driving to work this morning on the highway. I looked to my right and saw a woman in a brand-new Acura doing about 80 mph with her face up close to her rear-view mirror. She was putting on makeup.
I looked away for a moment and next thing I know she's halfway over in my lane, still working on her face.
It scared me so much that I dropped my electric shaver, which knocked the bacon roll out of my other hand.
In the confusion of trying to straighten the car using my knees on the steering wheel, I lost the Bluetooth from my ear. It fell into the coffee between my legs, where it splashed and burned my privates.
I yelled in pain and the cigarette fell out of my mouth, burning my shirt.
I also lost an important call.

What wears glass slippers and weighs 3,000 pounds?
Cinderellaphant.

Cat's favorite song: Three Blind Mice

An elderly man was having breakfast at a truck stop when three Hell's Angels bikers strutted in. The first biker put out his cigar in the man's scrambled eggs and then took a seat at the counter. The second biker squirted tobacco juice into the old man's orange juice and then took a seat at the counter. The third biker pretended to trip and bumped so hard that the old man fell forward into his breakfast plate. That biker then took a seat at the counter.
The old man cleaned himself off with a napkin, paid his bill and left the diner without a look or a word to the bikers.
A few minute after he left, one of the bikers said to the waitress: "Not much of a man, is he?" and laughed.
She replied: "Not much of a truck driver, either. He just backed his truck over three motorcycles."

Late at night, a drunk was on his knees under a streetlight, looking for something. A passerby asks if he could help. "I'm looking for my watch." "Just where do you think you lost it?" "Oh back a couple of blocks." "Then why in hell are you looking for it here?" "Because the light's better."

This guy marches into a bar and shouts, "A double whisky, please, barman, and a drink for everyone here ... and that includes you!"

"Thank you, sir," says the bartender and pours all the drinks.

Moments later, the guy calls out the same order. So the bartender says, "Pardon me, sir, but don't you think you should pay for the first round before you order another?"

The guy laughs and says, "I can't! I don't have any money!" He is obviously drunk.

The bartender is furious and orders the guy out of his bar. Twenty minutes later, the guy is back, yelling, "A double whisky for me and a drink for all my friends here!"

"I suppose you'll be offering me a drink, too:" sneers the barman.

"Not likely," says the guy. "You get real nasty when you've had a drink."

A man is in the Post Office, meticulously putting "Love" stamps on pink envelopes. Then he sprays cologne over them.
A curious bystander asks him what he's doing.
"I'm sending out 1,000 valentines signed 'Guess Who?' He's asked why he'd do that. "I'm a divorce lawyer."

Jon took the Staten Island ferry to and from Manhattan every day. One evening, he missed his usual boat and decided to have just one drink at a nearby bar. One drink turned into four or five and he was really flying. When he got to the ferry slip, the boat was about eight feet away. He took a running leap and landed right on the deck. "How about that jump?" he said to a deck hand, proudly.
"It was great," said the sailor. "But why didn't you wait for us to stop pulling in?"

A guy sits at a bar and orders six vodkas. The barman says, "Rough day?"
"Yeah, I found out my younger brother is gay." The barman clucks sympathetically. The very next day, the same man comes back and order six more shots of vodka. The barman says: "What's wrong today?"
"I found out my older brother is gay, too."
"Gee, that's pretty tough."
The next day, the guy is back again ordering six vodka shots. "Gee, man," he says, Another rough day?" The guy nods and drinks his shots down. The barman says, "Does anyone in your family like women?"
"Yeah," says the guy. "My wife."

TECH SUPPORT: A THANKLESS JOB?

TECH: What kind of computer do you have?
CALLER: It's a silver one.

CALLER: I can't get my DVD out!
TECH: Have you pushed the button all the way in?
CALLER: Yes. I'm sure it's really stuck.
TECH: That doesn't sound good. I'll put you through to my supervisor.
CALLER: No, wait a minute. I hadn't inserted it yet. It's on my desk... sorry!

CALLER: Good afternoon, I can't print. Every time I try, it says "CAN'T FIND PRINTER." I even lifted the printer and placed it in front of the monitor, but the computer still says it can't find it!

CALLER: I can't get on the Internet.
TECH: Are you absolutely sure you used the correct password?
CALLER: Yes, I'm sure. I saw my co-worker do it and she got on.
TECH: Can you tell me that password?
CALLER: Sure. Five dots.

USELESS FACTS

If you yelled for eight years, seven months and 6 days straight, you'd have produced enough sound energy to heat one cup of coffee.

Banging your head against the wall uses 150 calories an hour.

The strongest muscle in the human body is the tongue.

Starfish don't have brains.

A cockroach will live nine days without its head, before it starves to death.

Butterflies taste with their feet.

An ant can lift 50 times its own weight, can pull 30 pounds it own weight and always falls over on its right side when intoxicated.

Polar bears are left-handed.

Right-handed people live, on average, nine years longer than lefties.

An Israeli soldier, newly on duty, asked the Commanding Officer for a 2-day pass.
"Are you crazy?" said the CO. "You just joined the Israeli Army and you already want a 3-day pass? You must do something spectacular for that recognition!"
The soldier was back a day later, and in an Arab tank!
The CO was really impressed. He asked, "How the hell did you do it?"
"Well, I jumped in one of our tanks and went toward the border. As I approached the border, I saw an Arab tank.
"I put up my white flag and the Arab tank driver put up his white flag. We both got out so we could speak.
"I said to the Arab soldier, 'Do you want to get a 3-day pass?'
"So we exchanged tanks!"

A woman walks into a bank and applies for a loan. Why does she need a loan, the loan officer wants to know. "I'm getting a divorce." Says the banker: "We don't give loans for divorces. We give loans only for real estate, automobiles, businesses, home improvements..." The woman says, "Well, this will certainly be a home improvement."

A LONG BUT HUMOROUS BAR JOKE

A man walks into the neighborhood bar, sits next to the only other patron, chats for a few minutes, then moves to the other end of the bar. "That guy over there," he says, "is a big complainer. I say life is good."
"Really?" says the barman. "What do you do for a living?"
"I make bets. I'll bet you $5 I can bite my right eye." The bartender says, "You're on." The guy takes out his glass eye and bites it.
"You win. I didn't know you had a glass eye," says the barman.
"I'll let you make it back. I'll bet you $10 I can bite my <u>left</u> eye."
The guy isn't blind, so the barman agrees. The guy then takes out his false teeth and clamps them on his left eye.
"Well, you won again. But I can't afford to lose any more bets. That's it, buddy."
"Tell you what," says the guy. "I'll bet you $20 that I can walk six feet away and pee in this bottle, which I'll leave on the bar. I won't miss by even a drop."
Well, figures the barkeep, there's no way!
"You're on, buddy," he says.

The guy walks six feet, drops his pants and proceeds to pee all over everything. He doesn't even come close to the bottle, never mind aiming it into the opening.
With this, the bartender starts laughing. "Well, that was a dumb bet," he says, "I knew you couldn't do it. You owe me $20."
Just then, the man at the other end of the bar passes out and falls to the floor.
The bartender rushes over. "I'd better call 911," he says. "He looks really bad. I wonder what happened?"
As he's picking up the phone, the betting guy says, "Oh, he'll be all right. I bet him a thousand dollars that I could pee all over the place and you'd just laugh about it."

The State of Mississippi cannot discriminate against the Ku Klux Klan if it wants to be part of the Adopt-A-Highway program.
The Supreme Court said so.
The Department of Transportation can't remove the KKK sign; but they have the right to name their highways.
The KKK is now regularly cleaning up a stretch of the newly named Rosa Parks Freeway!
Someone there has a sense of humor.

ONE HUNDRED YEARS AGO IN THE U.S....

Average life expectancy was 47 years.

Only 14% of all homes had a bathtub; only 8% had a telephone.

The population of Las Vegas was 30.

Sugar cost 4 cents a pound. Eggs were 14 cents a dozen. Coffee: 15 cents a pound.

More than 95% of all births took place at home.

One in ten adults couldn't read or write. Only 6% were graduates of High School.

There was no Mother's or Father's Day.

18% of all households had at least one full-time servant.

The maximum speed limit in most cities was 10 mph.

There were only 8,000 cars in use and only 144 miles of paved roads.

An elderly, blind cowboy wanders into an all-girl biker bar by mistake. He finds his way to a bar stool and orders a shot of bourbon.
After a while, he calls to the bar: "Anyone wanna hear a blonde joke?"
The bar immediately falls silent.
In a calm voice, the woman next to the cowboy says,
"Before you tell that joke, cowboy, I think is only fair—since you are blind—that you know five things.
1. The bartender is a blonde girl with a baseball bat.
2. The bouncer is a blonde with a billy club—and she knows how to use it.
3. I'm a 6 foot, 165 pounds blonde with a black belt in karate.
4. The woman next to me is blonde and a weightlifter.
5. The lady to your left is blonde and a professional wrestler.
"Now think about it, cowboy. Do you still wanna tell that blonde joke?"
The blind cowboy thinks for a moment, shakes his head and mutters, "No... not if I'm gonna have to explain it five times."

The wages of sin is alimony.

A couple went shopping for Christmas at the local mall. It was packed.

As the wife made her way through the crowd, she turned back to make sure her husband was with her. He was not.

She was quite upset; they had a lot of shopping to do. And she couldn't figure how she had lost him so quickly. Maybe something was wrong. Maybe he had a heart attack.

Now she had put herself into a panic. She called him on her cellphone and when he answered, said, "I was so worried. I thought something awful had happened."

In a calm voice, he said, "Honey, you remember that jewelry store we went into about five years ago and you fell in love with a sapphire ring that we couldn't afford and I told you that one day I would get it for you?"

She choked up, and said, "Yes, I remember that jewelry store."

He said, "Well, I'm in the bar right next door."

It's a natural law:
Whatever hits the fan will NOT be distributed evenly.

CRAZY LAWS IN THESE UNITED STATES

In Indiana, citizens are not allowed to go to a movie or a theater, nor ride in a public bus for 4 hours after eating garlic.

Mourners at a wake in Massachusetts may not eat more than three sandwiches.

In Iowa, a law says kisses may last for as much as, but no longer than, 5 minutes.

Women in Florida can be fined for falling asleep under the hairdryer in a salon.

The meanest State in the Union: Washington State bans lollipops altogether.

You may not cross the street standing on your hands if you are in Connecticut.

Kentucky says it's illegal to transport an ice cream cone in your pocket.

How about this for unfair? Beer and pretzels cannot be served at the same time in North Dakota in any bar or restaurant.

A lady named Ann Rosenberg was stranded many years ago when her car broke down. She was within walking distance of a resort—one which did not admit Jews. When she told the front desk clerk her name, he said, "Sorry, the hotel is full."
"But the sign outside says you have vacancies."
The desk clerk stammered a moment, then said bluntly, "You know that we do not admit Jews to this hotel."
"I'll have you know," said Mrs. R., "that I have converted to your religion."
"Really?" said the clerk. "Okay, take a little test. How was Jesus born?"
"He was born to a virgin named Mary in a little town called Bethlehem."
"Not bad," said the clerk. "Continue."
Mrs. Rosenberg said, "He was born in a manger."
"And why was he born in a manger?"
She answered loudly: "Because a jerk like you wouldn't give a Jewish lady a room for the night!"

Why is sex like software?
For every person who pays for it, there are hundreds who get it for free.

Moses and his Israelites have just escaped from bondage and they arrive at the sea, with the Egyptians in hot pursuit.
Moses calls a staff meeting.
Moses: Well, how are we going to get across that sea? We need a fast solution.
General of the Armies: Normally, I'd recommend that we build a pontoon bridge to carry us across. But there's not enough time. The Egyptians are too close.
Admiral of the Navy: Normally, I'd recommend that we build barges to float us across; but time is too short.
Moses: Does <u>anyone</u> have a solution?
The Public Relations Guy: No, but I can promise you this: if you find a way out of this one, I can get you two or three pages in the Old Testament.

A man bought a new car, which he loved, and was somewhat reluctant to let his wife drive this prized possession even to the grocery store two blocks away.
But she kept insisting and he finally relented, saying, "Remember, if you have an accident, the newspaper will print your age."

You can't judge a book by its movie.

WHY DOGS ARE BETTER THAN WOMEN

Dogs love it when your friends come over.

Dogs don't hate their bodies.

Your dog's parents never visit.

Dogs will forgive you for playing with other dogs.

Dogs don't care if you use their shampoo.

Dogs think you sing great.

Dogs don't shop.

Dogs never expect gifts.

Dogs don't worry about germs.

You never have to wait for a dog. They're ready 24/7.

Dogs never borrow your shirts.

Dogs seldom outlive you.

In a third world country a priest, a lawyer and an engineer are sentenced to die by guillotine.
The priest kneels and puts his head on the block, they pull the rope, and nothing happens. He declares he's been saved by divine intervention and he is let go.
The lawyer kneels, puts his head on the block, they pull the rope and again, nothing happens. He claims he can't be executed twice for the same crime, so he is set free.
The engineer is grabbed, pushed to his knees, his head forced down. He looks up at the release mechanism and says,
"Wait a minute. I see your problem."

One night a fellow drove his secretary home after she got tipsy at an office party. He didn't tell his wife, who got jealous easily. The next night, the man and wife were driving to a party. At a red light, he spotted a high heel shoe half hidden under the other seat. When his wife was looking out the window, he grabbed it and tossed it out of the car. Relieved, he pulled into the restaurant parking lot. Then he saw his wife was squirming in her seat, looking. "Honey," she said, "did you see my other shoe?"

Howard was invited for dinner at a friend's house. He'd never met this friend's wife, who seemed very sweet. And Howard was quite impressed at how his host preceded every request with an endearment: "Honey, could we have the butter," and "Darling, please pass the salt," and "Sweetheart, can we have another bottle of wine?"
While she was in the kitchen getting dessert, Howard said, "It's really very nice that after all the years you've been married, you still call her those pet names."
The host said softly: "Can I be honest? "I've forgotten her name."

A woman went to the doctor's office for an annual exam. She was seen by one of the younger doctors in the practice and after a few minutes, she came out of the room, screaming. The receptionist had the head doctor speak to her. Then he went to see the young doctor. "You were giving this lady a physical," he said. "She's 68 years old and a grandmother. What in hell were you thinking of, telling her she's pregnant? That was stupid!"
The young doctor smiled and said, "Cured her hiccups, though, didn't it?"

Monica saw that her friend Gladys had eyes red from crying. "What's wrong?" she asked. "My husband has left me." "Left you! But you two were so perfect for each other. Why did he leave??
"It's the television's fault. He saw a commercial that said 'Drink Canada Dry;' and now he's gone to see if he can do it!"

A man saw that his best friend was down in the mouth, and asked him what his problem was. "My wife enrolled me in a bridge club," was the answer. "That doesn't sound so bad," said the man. His friend replied, "I didn't think so, either. And then I found that I'm scheduled to jump off next Thursday."

An avid duck hunter was amazed to discover that one of his dogs could walk on water. He decided not to tell but to <u>show</u> his friend the scientist that this was a fact. The two men went duck hunting and, sure enough, every time a duck was down, the dog walked daintily on the water to retrieve it. The scientist said nothing. On the way home, he was asked if he'd noticed anything. "I sure did," he said. "Your dog can't swim."

A woman goes into a pet shop and says she wants a pet that can do everything. Not a cat, not a dog. No, she wants a pet that can do everything she wants. The owner thinks for a while and then suggests a centipede.

"A centipede?" she says. "I don't see it, but okay, give me your best centipede."

At home, the new pet owner tells the centipede to clean the kitchen. The centipede disappears and half an hour later, the kitchen is a clean and shining glory. Wow! she thinks, this is great. "Now clean the living room," she says. Thirty minutes later, the living room is fresh and clean, pillows plumped and plants watered.

The amazed woman thinks: this is really amazing. I am a lucky woman!

Next, she says to the centipede, "Run down to the corner and bring me back today's newspaper."

The centipede leaves. Ten minutes later... no paper. Twenty minutes later... no paper. Now she's worried. She runs to the front door, opens it... and there's the centipede sitting on the top step. "Hey!!" she says. "I sent you out a long time ago. What's up?"

"I'm going, I'm going," says the centipede. "I'm just putting on my shoes."

A flying saucer landed at a gas station on a lonely country road. The two aliens seemed completely unconcerned about being spotted. In fact, their shiny craft was emblazoned with the letters UFO. The station owner was paralyzed with shock, but not his young blond gas jockey, who nonchalantly filled their tank, took their money, and waved them off.
"Do you realize what just happened?" the owner finally managed to say.
"Yeah," says the blond guy. "So?"
"Those were aliens from space!"
"Yeah, so?"
"Didn't you notice the letters UFO on the side of their vehicle?"
"Yeah, so?"
"Don't you realize what UFO means?"
The blond kid rolled his eyes. "Geez, boss," he said, "of course I know what UFO means. Unleaded Fuel Only."

We are becoming lesser by the day. You want proof?
Our communication: wireless. Our dress: topless. Our politicians: feckless. Our telephones: cordless. Our drivers: reckless. Our cooking: fireless. Our youth: jobless.

A lawyer finds out that he has a brain tumor, and it's inoperable. In fact, it's so large, they will have to do a complete brain transplant. His doctor gives him the choice of available brains. There's a jar of rocket scientist brains for $15 an ounce and a jar of lawyer brains for the princely sum of $800 an ounce.
The outraged lawyer says, "This is a ripoff! How come the lawyer brains are so damned expensive?"
The doctor says, "Do you know how many lawyers it takes to get an ounce of brain?"

Two guys are in a bar on the 20th floor. One guy says, "Bet you $100 I can jump out the window and right back in."
The second guy thinks he's got an easy $100; but sure enough, the other man jumps out the window and, a moment later, jumps back in. He does this twice more, and each time more money is bet. The second man figures there's a freak wind out there so he bets $500 he can do it, too.
The first man agrees and watches as the guy jumps out the window and falls to his death. The barman says, "Gee, you can be a real SOB when you drink, Superman."

Nine Things You'd Love to Say at Work (but won't)

I can see your point, but I still think you're full of crap.

I have plenty of talent and vision. I just don't give a damn.

How about "never?" Is never good for you?

It sounds like Engish, but I don't understand a single word you're saying.

I see you've set aside a special time to humiliate yourself in public.

Aha! I see the mess-up fairy has visited us.

You are validating my inherent distrust of co-workers.

Are you coming on to me or just having a seizure?

The fact that no one gets you does not mean that you're an artist.

The state of Arizona has no Daylight Savings Time because they listened to the wise old Indian. After having Daylight Savings Time explained, the old Indian said, "Only a white man would believe that you can cut a foot off the top of a blanket and sew it to the bottom of a blanket and have a longer blanket."

An attorney telephoned the governor just after midnight, wishing to speak with him regarding a matter of utmost urgency.
An aide finally agreed to wake the governor. "So, what's so important?" grumped the sleepy governor. "Judge Garber has just died," said the lawyer, "and I want to take his place."
Replied the governor, "Well, it's okay with me if it's okay with the undertaker."

Kids who never come when called will grow up to be doctors. Kids who come before they are called will grow up to be lawyers.

My friend and I were in front of a fast-food joint that had a sign saying "No bills larger than $20 accepted." My friend said, "If I had more than $20, I wouldn't eat here.

A father put his 3-year-old daughter to bed. She said, "God bless Mommy and Daddy and Grandma and bye-bye, Grandpa." Why bye-bye? She didn't know. But the next day, Grandpa passed away. A week later, she asked God to bless Mommy and Daddy and said bye-bye to Grandma. Sure enough, Grandma died a few days later. Then came the night when she said, "God bless Mommy and bye-bye, Daddy." Well, Daddy nearly went into shock. He felt doomed. He couldn't sleep at all that night and was totally unnerved all day at the office, waiting for...something...to happen to him. He figured if he made it to midnight, then he was okay and the other two deaths were just coincidences. He stayed at the office until the midnight hour had passed and then, greatly relieved, went home.

His wife said, "What kept you so late?"

He said, "I really don't want to talk about it, but I've just spent the worst day of my life."

His wife said, "You think you had a bad day? You'll never believe what happened to me.

"This morning, right in the middle of my lesson, my golf pro dropped dead!"

A golfer hooked his tee shot over a hill and onto the next fairway. Walking toward his ball, he saw a man on the ground, curled up and moaning with pain.
As he approached the fallen man, the man looked up at him and said, between clenched teeth: "I'm an attorney and this is going to cost you $5,000."
"I'm really sorry," said the concerned golfer, "But I did say 'fore!'"
"I'll take it!" said the man on the ground.

Because they had no reservation at a popular restaurant, an older couple were told they'd have to wait 45 minutes for a table. "Young man," said the elderly gentleman, "we're in our 90s. We might not HAVE 45 minutes."
They were seated immediately.

Juan and Carlos are both broke and both panhandling. Carlos has bought a new car, new clothes and is doing very well, but Juan only collects a few dollars each day. Carlos says, "Look at your sign. It says you have a wife and 6 kids to support. Look at my sign." Carlos's sign says: I ONLY NEED ANOTHER $10 TO MOVE BACK TO MEXICO.

An old man goes to the local wizard and asks if he can remove a curse the man's been living with for 40 years.
The wizard says, "Maybe. But I'll have to know the exact words used to put the curse on you."
"Oh, I know the exact words. 'I now pronounce you man and wife.'"

A man came home one evening to find his wife in a sexy negligee. "Tie me up," she purred, "and you can do anything you like." So he tied her up and went fishing.

A drunk phoned the police to report a theft. "It's my car! They've taken the dashboard, the steering wheel...everything!" A few minutes later, he called back to say he'd got into the back seat by mistake.

An amoeba named Sam and his brother
Were having a drink with each other.
In the midst of their quaffing,
They split themselves laughing
And each of them now is a mother.

One night, there was a loud knocking on the front door. The man of the house answered. Nobody was there. And then he noticed a tiny snail on the doormat. He picked it up and threw it all the way across the street into a vacant lot.

A year later, there was a loud knocking on the front door. Once again, the man went to answer and once again, nobody was to be seen. Then he looked down and there was the same snail.

The snail said, "What the hell was THAT all about?"

The Kindergarten teacher was observing her class as they drew pictures for their art period. One little girl, she noticed, was working very diligently, totally absorbed in her work.

"What are you drawing?" asked the teacher.

The little girl said, "God."

The teacher paused and then said, God? But, you know, we don't know what God looks like."

Without missing a beat or looking up from her artwork, the little girl said,

"They will in a minute."

A man and woman had been married for more than 60 years. They had shared everything. They had discussed everything. They had kept no secrets, except that the old woman had a shoe box in the top of her closet that she had cautioned her husband never to look at or ask her about.

Well, the time came when the old lady was sick and the doctor felt she would not recover. About to die, she told her husband he could now take down the shoebox and see what was in it.

When he opened it, he found two crocheted dolls, very nice ones, and a stack of money totaling $95,000.

He asked her about the contents, and she told him that when they were to be married, her mother told her never to argue, but every time she got mad at her husband, she should crochet a doll.

He was very moved; only two dolls were in the box. In all those years, only two crocheted dolls to show her anger.

"Darling," he said, "that's such a lovely story. But where did all that money come from?"

"Oh, that," she said. "That's what I made from selling the dolls."

Mike liked his drink a bit too much. Every Saturday he would go to the local sports bar, watch a game, and drink. Usually, one of his friends would stop him before he drank too much; but this football game was really great and it went into overtime

And Mike kept ordering another and another.

Finally, the bartender said, "No more for you, Mike." And turned to look at the game.

"Okay, I'll be on my way then."

He climbed off his bar stool and fell flat on his face.

He took a step toward the door and fell again. Nobody noticed him because all eyes were on the TV. He figured he just needed some fresh air. He was near the front door, so out he went. He took one step and fell again. He figured he must really be drunk.

His house was not far away and so, walking and falling and crawling, he made his way home. He crawled into his bedroom and hoisted himself into bed.

The next morning, his wife came in with a cup of coffee for him. She said, "You must have had a lot to drink last night."

"I did," he admitted. "How did you know?"

"The bartender called. You forgot your wheelchair."

A load of politicians were in a bus going down a country road, when the bus suddenly went off the road and crashed into a farmer's barn. The old farmer got off his tractor and went to investigate.
Soon, he dug a big hole and buried them. A few days later, the local sheriff came out to investigate. He saw the crashed bus and he asked the farmer where all the politicians were. "Washington has the FBI and the CIA and everyone out looking for them," he said. The farmer told him he'd buried them. "Good lord, were they ALL dead?" asked the sheriff. The farmer said, "Well, some of them said they weren't, but you know how them crooked politicians lie!"

Spanish singer Julio Iglesias was on television with a British host, when he used the word "manyana." The host asked what it meant. He said, "It's a term that means the job will be done maybe tomorrow, maybe the next day, maybe the day after that, who cares?" The host turned to Irishman Shay Brennan who was also a guest and asked for an equivalent in Irish. "No, in Ireland we don't have a word to describe that degree of urgency."

Sister Mary Katherine entered the Order of Silence. The Mother Superior said to her, "This is the Order of Silence. We never speak, we even whisper our prayers. You are welcome to join us, but you must not speak unless I direct you to do so."
Sister Mary Katherine agreed. She was in the convent for five years when the Mother Superior paid her a visit.
"You may now say two words," she said.
"Hard bed," said Sister Mary Katherine.
"I'll see what I can do," said the Mother Superior.
Five more years went by and once again, Sister Mary Katherine was told she could speak two words.
"Terrible food," she said.
"I'll look into that," said the Mother Superior. At the fifteen-year mark, once again Sister Mary Katherine was visited by the Mother Superior and told she might say two words. These were her words:
"I quit."
"It's probably for the best," said the Mother Superior.
"You've done nothing but bitch since you got here."

SIGNS AND SLOGANS

The Ultimate Bathroom Joke Book

If you can read this, thank a teacher. And, since it's in English, thank a soldier.

May your life someday be as awesome as you pretend it is on Facebook.

DON'T VOTE. IT ONLY ENCOURAGES THEM.

WILL THE PERSON WHO TOOK THE STEPLADDER YESTERDAY PLEASE RETURN IT OR FURTHER STEPS WILL BE TAKEN.

Health Food Store: CLOSED DUE TO ILLNESS

BARGAIN BASEMENT UPSTAIRS

Toilet out of order...please use floor below.

WE CAN REPAIR ANYTHING. (Please knock hard on the door. The bell doesn't work.)

THE FARMER ALLOWS PEOPLE TO CROSS THE FIELD FREE...BUT THE BULL CHARGES

ELEPHANTS! PLEASE STAY IN YOUR CAR

WORKERS OF THE WORLD... GET A LIFE!

The Ultimate Bathroom Joke Book

Jesus is coming! Look busy!

The first two husbands are just for practice!

SIGN ON AN OFFICE DESK: You have a right to your opinion and I have a right to tell you how stupid it is.

Take notice! When this sign is under water, the road is impassable.

You are welcome to visit the cemetery where famous Russian and Soviet composers, artists and writers are buried daily, except Thursday.

Shop sign in Abu Dahbi: IF THE FRONT IS CLOSED, PLEASE ENTER THROUGH MY BACK SIDE.

Press any key to start. Where in hell is the ANY key?

MOST EXCLUSIVE DISCO IN TOWN! EVERYONE WELCOME

DON'T DRINK AND DRIVE. You might hit a bump and spill something.

SIGN ON A CITY STREET TRAFFIC LIGHT:

DON'T WALK. DANCE.

Don't worry about your health. It'll go away.

A clear conscience is the sign of fuzzy memory.

Billboard: Fishmore & Doolittle, Retirement Planning and Consultants

DIAPERS & POLITICIANS SHOULD BE CHANGED OFTEN...BOTH FOR THE SAME REASON

Sometimes I pretend to be NORMAL. But it gets boring and I go back to being me.

SARCASM: Because beating the crap out of people is illegal.

I have PMS & GPS
Which means I am a bitch and I can find you.

I don't have an attitude. I have a personality you can't handle.

Claustrophobia: fear of Santa Claus

I hide behind sarcasm because telling you to go screw yourself is considered rude in most situations.

Airline ticket office sign in Copenhagen: WE TAKE YOUR BAGS AND SEND THEM IN ALL DIRECTIONS.

Cocktail lounge, Norway: LADIES ARE REQUESTED NOT TO HAVE CHILDREN IN THE BAR

ON A POSTER: Are you an adult that cannot read? If so, contact us. We can help.

Japanese hotel: Guests are requested not to smoke, or do other disgusting things in the beds.

Honk if you love Jesus. Text if you want to meet him.

I love it when my pills kick in!

A hotel in Japan: YOU ARE INVITED TO TAKE ADVANTAGE OF THE CHAMBERMAID.

A sign in Germany. The Germans are always thorough.
IT IS STRICTLY FORBIDDEN ON OUR CAMPING SITE THAT PEOPLE OF DIFFERENT SEX, FOR INSTANCE, MEN AND WOMEN, LIVE TOGETHER IN ONE TENT, UNLESS THEY ARE MARRIED WITH EACH OTHER FOR THIS PURPOSE.

Learn from your parents' mistakes. USE BIRTH CONTROL.

Seen at a business conference:
FOR ANYONE WHO HAS CHILDREN AND DON'T KNOW IT, THERE IS A DAY CARE ON THE FIRST FLOOR

IN A SAIGON BAR: Special cocktails for the ladies with nuts.

Seen in a London office: AFTER TEA BREAK, STAFF SHOULD EMPTY TEAPOT AND STAND UPSIDE DOWN ON THE DRAINING BOARD.

The first 40 years of childhood are the worst.

The first 5 days after the weekend are always the hardest.

WOULD YOU LIKE TO RIDE YOUR OWN ASS? (donkey ride in Thailand)

Hotel in Zurich:
Because of the impropriety of entertaining guests of the opposite sex in the bedroom, it is suggested that the lobby be used for this purpose.

In a Laundromat:
AUTOMATIC WASHING MACHINES. PLEASE REMOVE ALL YOUR CLOTHES WHEN THE WATER GOES OUT.

SIGN IN A GERONTOLOGIST'S OFFICE:
Senior citizens are like sharks.
If they stop moving….
They die.

Graffiti: History repeats itself, but each time the price goes up.

On a t-shirt: Were you standing in the shallow end of the gene pool?

On a taxidermy office door: WE KNOW OUR STUFF

Written on a wall: Don't take life so seriously. It isn't permanent.

On another wall: If you're going to go onto thin ice, you might as well dance.

I DO WHATEVER MY RICE KRISPIES TELL ME TO DO

If you want help from the U.S. government ... move to another country!

God grant me the serenity to accept things I cannot change, the courage I need to change the things I can, and the weaponry to make it possible.

Work is the price you pay for money.

THE TROUBLE WITH TROUBLE SHOOTING IS THAT TROUBLE SHOOTS BACK.

If you can't live without me, why aren't you dead yet?

When marriage is outlawed, only outlaws will have in-laws.

Women like cats. Men like dogs.

The Ultimate Bathroom Joke Book

In a ladies' room: In this world, it rains on the Just and the Unjust...but the Unjust have the Just's umbrella.

In a dressing room: Excuse me while I change into something more formidable.

Graffiti: There's a thin woman inside every fat one. I ate mine.

I eat junk food to get it out of the house.

The ozone layer or cheese in a spray can? Don't make me choose!

Outside a muffler shop: No appointment necessary. We can hear you coming.

Sign seen at a car dealership: Best way to get back on your feet? Miss a car payment.

Maternity room door sign:
Push. Push. Push.

Coffee is my only true friend.

Tire shop sign: Invite us to your next blowout!

PLEASE DO NOT SMOKE NEAR THE GAS PUMPS. MAYBE YOUR LIFE'S NOT WORTH MUCH, BUT OUR GAS IS.

In a non-smoking area: If we see smoke, we will assume you are on fire and will take appropriate action.

Seen on a septic tank truck: YESTERDAY'S MEALS ON WHEELS

In front of a church: 7 days without God makes one weak.

On a plumber's truck: WE REPAIR WHAT YOUR HUSBAND FIXED

In an oculist's office: If you don't see what you want, you've come to the right place.

In a vet's waiting room:
BACK SOON. SIT! STAY!

Sign in the front yard of a funeral home: DRIVE CAREFULLY. WE'LL WAIT.

Nature abhors a vacuum. And so do I.

The harder you fall, the higher you bounce.

BUMPER STICKERS SEEN HERE AND THERE

Boldly going nowhere.

I haven't lost my mind...it's backed up on disk somewhere.

It's been lovely but I have to scream now.

The face is familiar but I can't quite remember my name.

Honk if anything falls off.

He Who Hesitates is Not Only Lost, but Miles from the next Exit.

Where are we going and why am I in this handbasket?

Traffic lights timed for 35 mph are also timed for 70 mph.

They say money doesn't buy happiness.
I SAY: NEITHER DOES BEING BROKE.

BUMPER STICKERS FOR WOMEN

So many men, so few who can afford me.

God made us sisters...Prozac made us friends.

WARNING: I have an attitude and I can use it.

If there's no chocolate in Heaven...I ain't goin'.

My mother is a travel agent for guilt trips.

Princess, having had quite enough experience with Princes, seeks frog.

Don't treat me any differently than you would the Queen.

If you want breakfast in bed, sleep in the kitchen.

COFFEE, CHOCOLATE, MEN...some things are just much better rich.

EVE WAS FRAMED.

Dinner is ready when the smoke alarm goes off.

DON'T HONK AT ME. I'M UPSET. I'M RUNNING OUT OF PLACES TO HIDE THE BODIES.

I don't question <u>your</u> existence. –GOD

If God didn't want us to eat animals, why did he make them out of meat?

SIGN IN A CHINESE PET STORE: Buy one dog, get one flea.

On a bar mirror: Money can't buy happiness but is sure makes misery easier to live with.

I don't like political jokes. I've seen too many of them get elected.

I'm a nobody and nobody is perfect; therefore, I am perfect.

It's okay, I didn't believe in reincarnation the last time.

You! Off my planet!

I'm in my own little world, but that's okay. They know me here.

Bumper sticker: When the Rapture comes, can I have your car?

In a men's room: Lord, help me to be the person my dog thinks I am.

The next time you think you're perfect ... try walking on water.

I pretend to work. They pretend to pay me.

If I throw a stick, will you leave?

I started out with nothing and still have most of it left.

Therapy is expensive. Popping bubble wrap is cheap. You choose.

Don't bother me. I'm living happily ever after.

Who are these kids and why are they calling me Mom?

Too many freaks...not enough circuses.

This isn't an office. It's Hell with fluorescent lighting.

The Ultimate Bathroom Joke Book

Well, this day was a total waste of makeup.

Seen in England: SLOW CATTLE CROSSING. NO PASSING FOR THE NEXT 100 YEARS.

QUICKSAND! Any person passing this point will be drowned.
By order of the Town Council.

Out to lunch. If not back by five, out to dinner, too

Outside a secondhand shop: WE EXCHANGE ANYTHING. BICYCLES, WASHING MACHINES, OLD COMPUTERS, ETC.
Why not bring your wife along and get a wonderful bargain!

Sign outside a new town hall: THE TOWN HALL IS CLOSED UNTIL OPENING. IT WILL REMAIN CLOSED AFTER BEING OPENED. OPEN TOMORROW.

Again, from England: DUE TO INCREASING PROBLEMS WITH LOCAL LOUTS AND VANDALS WE MUST ASK ANYONE WITH RELATIVES BURIED IN THE GRAVEYARD TO DO THEIR BEST TO KEEP THEM IN ORDER.

Horse Manure. $3 per pre-packed bag; $1 do-it-yourself.

On a church door: This is the Gate of Heaven. Enter ye all by this door.
(This door is kept locked because of the draft. Please use side door.)

A dry cleaner's sign: ANYONE LEAVING THEIR GARMENTS HERE FOR MORE THAN 30 DAYS WILL BE DISPOSED OF.

On a t-shirt: Ask me about my vow of silence.

On a rest room wall: I'd like to take you out. And leave you there.

The Lottery...you have to play to lose.

In dog years...I'M DEAD!

DYSLEXICS HAVE MORE NUF!

On a t-shirt: If it's any of your business, it ain't gossip.

On a bar mirror: Don't hate yourself in the morning. Sleep till noon.

COMMON SENSE IS LIKE DEODORANT. The people who need it most never use it.

IT'S FUNNY HOW WHEN I'M LOUD, PEOPLE TELL ME TO BE QUIET. BUT WHEN I'M QUIET, PEOPLE ASK ME WHAT'S WRONG.

Posted in a ladies' room: It's better to have loved and lost then to live with the psycho for the rest of your life.

Am I getting older, or has the supermarket begun playing great music?

SOMEBODY STOLE MY IDENTITY LAST WEEK. TODAY, THEY SHOWED UP AT MY DOOR AND PLEADED WITH ME TO TAKE IT BACK.

A small boy asks: Why is it the poop deck?

BUMPER STICKERS WE'VE SEEN LATELY

I THINK, THEREFORE I'M OVERQUALIFIED

I am in shape. ROUND is a shape.

I don't repeat gossip. So listen carefully.

I LIKE POINTY THINGS.

I'm leaving my body to science-fiction.

I may have Alzheimer's but thank God I don't have Alzheimer's.

EVERYTHING I NEEDED TO KNOW, I LEARNED IN PRISON

YOU LAUGH BECAUSE I'M DIFFERENT.
I laugh because the Zorgons command it.

I've seen NORMAL. It ain't pretty.

I'm one of those BAD things that happen to GOOD people

ADRENALINE is my drug of choice.

If it weren't for the gutter, my mind would be homeless.

If they don't have chocolate in heaven, I ain't goin'!

I'm not as think as you confused I am.

MY MIND'S MADE UP. Kindly do not confuse me with the facts

I WOULD NEVER LEAD YOU ASTRAY. I reserve the right, however, to follow you there

I'M CANADIAN. It's like American but without the gun

VENI VIDI VISTA
I came, I saw, I shopped.

The ABE diet. Anything But Exercise

You nonconformists are all alike!

REALITY IS NICE...BUT I WOULDN'T WANT TO LIVE THERE

I don't hate you. I just hope your next period happens in a shark tank.

A law of life: you can't fall off the floor.

The future isn't what it used to be.

On a t-shirt: I'm too young to be this old.

Posted on an airport bathroom mirror: If we were meant to fly, we wouldn't lose our luggage.

You're only young once. After that, you need a different excuse.

Ignorance is bliss. But it'll never replace sex.

On a bumper sticker: Complex problems have easy to understand wrong answers.

Graffiti: I found Jesus. He said, Tag, you're it!

Bumper sticker: I work to get away from my cat

Graffiti: Give me levity or give me death!

Inflation is when the buck doesn't stop anywhere.

Wives are people who feel they don't dance enough.

My idea of housework is to sweep the room with a glance.

REAL HEADLINES FROM REAL NEWSPAPERS

Hospitals resort to hiring doctors.

Man with eight DUIs blames drinking problem

Homicide victims rarely talk to police.

Barbershop singers bring joy to school for the deaf.

New sick policy require 2-day notice

Parents keep kids home to protest school closure

Rally against apathy draws small crowd

The bra celebrates a pair of historic milestones this year

Total lunar eclipse will be broadcast live on Northwoods Public Radio

Miracle cure kills fifth patient

Rangers get whiff of Colon

Yet More Bumper Stickers...

I don't suffer from insanity. I enjoy every minute of it.

Earth is the insane asylum for the Universe.

I took an IQ test and the results were negative.

To all you virgins, thanks for nothing.

I used to have a handle on life, but it broke.

I'm not a complete idiot. Some parts are missing.

BEER-the reason I get up every afternoon.

Beauty is in the eye of the beer holder.

Consciousness: that annoying time between naps.

I don't have to be dead to donate my organ.

RAT—the other white meat.

A Tennessee cop pulled over a drunk driver. "Got an I.D.?" he said. "'Bout what?"

INTERESTING WARNING SIGNS

On an infant bathtub:
Do not throw baby out with bath water.

On a piano:
Harmful or fatal if swallowed.

On work gloves:
for best results, do not leave at crime scene.

On a children's wooden block set:
Letters may be used to construct words, phrases and sentences that may be deemed offensive.

On shoe Odor Eaters:
DO NOT EAT

On a blender:
Not to be used as an aquarium!

On a disposable razor:
not for use during an earthquake.

On a roll of Life Savers:
Not for use as a flotation device

The Ultimate Bathroom Joke Book

SHORT AND SASSY

The Ultimate Bathroom Joke Book

The Cadbury Candy Company and Merck Drug Company have combined to market the new mint-flavored birth control pill that women may take immediately before sex. The pill will be distributed by the large drug store chains and will be called:
Pre-Dick-a-Mints.

One of the questions from the U.S. Navy Aviation career placement test given to applicants was:
"Rearrange the letters P N E S I to spell out an important part of the human body that is more useful when erect."
All those who spelled SPINE became doctors. The rest went to Pensacola for Flight School.

My girlfriend and I went to the pub for some beers and the local idiots were shouting "pedophile" at me, just because my girlfriend is 21 and I'm 50.
It completely spoiled our 10th anniversary.

The cost of living has gotten so bad that my wife is having sex with me because she can't afford batteries.

Life is about kicking ass ... not kissing it.

My wife suggested I get a penis enlarger, so I did. She's 21 and her name is Lucy.

A man calls 911 and shouts, "I think my wife is dead!" The operator says, "What makes you think that?"
He says, "The sex is the same, but the ironing is beginning to pile up."

Women always say that giving birth is way more painful for them than a guy getting kicked in the nuts. They are so wrong! A year or two after giving birth, some women will say, "It would be so nice to have another baby."
No matter how much time goes by, you'll never hear a guy say, "Gee, I'd like another kick in the nuts!"

Son: Mommy, when I was on the bus with Daddy this morning, he told me to give up my seat to a lady.
Mom: Well, that's the right thing to do, honey.
Son: But, Mommy, I was sitting on his lap!

Whoever named it necking didn't know his anatomy.

An elderly man goes into a brothel. He says he's 90 years old. "Ninety!" exclaims the madam. "Don't you realize you've had it?" "So sorry," he says. "How much do I owe you?"

My son was thrown out of school today for letting a girl in his class give him a hand-job. I said, "Son, that's three schools this year! You'd better stop before you're banned from teaching altogether!"

I've heard that Apple has scrapped their plans for the new child-oriented iPod after realizing that "iTouch Kids" is really not a good name.

A worried wife was told by her husband's doctor that her husband was dying. "Can't you save him, doctor?" she cried. "I cannot," said the doctor, "but you can. Simply give him oral sex."
"Oral sex? I have to give him oral sex?"
"Yes."
"And oral sex will save him?" Yes.
The woman went home. Her husband asked what the doctor had said.
"He says you're dying."

There once was a couple called Kelly
Who walked around belly to belly
Because, in their haste,
They used library paste
Instead of petroleum jelly.

The lab calls Mrs. Smith and says they're very sorry, but somehow Mr. Smith's bloods got mixed up with another man's. One man has syphilis and the other, Alzheimer's. "Oh dear, what should I do?" she says.
"When he comes home, send him out for milk. If he comes back with it, don't screw him."

OFFICIAL ANNOUNCEMENT
The government today announced that it is changing its emblem from an eagle to a condom because the condom more accurately reflects the government's political stance.
A condom allows for inflation, halts production, destroys the next generation, protects a bunch of dicks, and gives you a sense of security while you're actually being screwed.
It just doesn't get more accurate than that!

At the start of an annual exam, the young doctor placed his stethoscope on the chest of an elderly woman.
"Big breaths," he instructed.
"Yes, they used to be," said she.

The doctor sadly informed the wife that her husband had had a massive myocardial infarct. She told the family he had died of a "massive internal fart."

A modern synagogue honors its Rabbi for 25 years of service by sending him to Hawaii for a week, all expenses paid. When he walks into his hotel room, he finds a beautiful nude woman lying on the bed. She says, "I'm a little something extra that the president of your congregation arranged."
The Rabbi is incensed. He picks up the phone and calls the President and shouts, "Rosenbaum, what were you thinking? Where is your respect? I am your moral leader! I'm very angry and you haven't heard the end of this!"
Hearing this, the woman gets up and starts to get dressed.
The Rabbi turns to her and says, "Where are you going? I'm not angry with you."

A newly married man asked his wife, "Would you have married me if my father hadn't left me a fortune?"
"Honey," his wife said sweetly, "I'd have married you no matter WHO left you a fortune!"

The 83-year-old woman was finished with her medical examination. The doctor said, "Miriam, do you and your husband still have intercourse?"
"Just a minute..." she said, and stepped out of the room. Loudly, she yelled, "Jerry, do we still have intercourse?"
There was a hush. You could hear a pin drop. Then he called back, "Miriam, for the one-hundredth time! We have BLUE CROSS!"

A woman worried that her husband was losing interest in sex. She decided to buy some crotchless panties she'd seen in a sex shop. That night, she put on a sexy negligee and the new panties. She strolled between her husband and the tv and put one leg up on the chair arm. "Want some of this?" she purred. "Are you crazy?" he replied. "Look what it did to your underwear!"

A young boy was coerced into giving the prayer before dinner. So he said, "Dear Lord, thank you for our visitors and their kids who finished all my cookies. Forgive our neighbor's son, who took off my sister's clothes and wrestled with her on her bed. And please give shelter to the homeless men who use Mommy's room when Daddy is at work. Amen."

There once was a man called Dave
Who kept a dead whore in a cave.
He said, "I admit
I'm a bit of a shit,
But think of the money I save."

A man walked into a confessional and said to the priest, "I'm 87, I have a wonderful wife, lovely children, perfect grandchildren and yet, last night when I met three biker girls , they took me to a motel and we screwed all night." The priest said, "Are you sorry for your sins?" "Sins? What sins?"
"What kind of Catholic are you, anyway?"
"I'm not Catholic," says the man. "I'm Jewish."
"Then why are you telling me these things?"
"I'm 87 years old. I'm telling everybody!"

A little girl wondered, "Where do babies come from?"
"From the stork," her Daddy lied.
"I know that!" she said impatiently. "What I want to know is, who screwed the stork?"

Woody Allen said: Last night I discovered a new kind of oral contraceptive. I asked a girl to go out with me and she said No.

Wife: What do you like most in me, my face or my body?
Husband: (after thought) Your sense of humor.

Making confession, Mary said, "I have sinned. My boyfriend and I made love seven times today."
The priest said, "Squeeze seven lemons into a glass of water and drink it down."
"Will this absolve me of my sin?"
"No, but it should wipe that smile off your face!"

My doctor told me I must stop masturbating. I asked her why.
"Because I'm trying to examine you."

A man is sitting quietly, reading the newspaper when his wife hits him with a folded newspaper all around his head. "What was THAT for?" he says. "That was for the piece of paper I found in your pants pocket, with the name Jenny written on it." He says, "When I was at the racetrack last week, Jenny was the name of a horse someone told me to bet." His wife apologizes and continues with whatever she's doing. Later that evening, the man is quietly watching TV when in storms his wife and this time she hits him with a broom. "Ow! And what's THAT for?" he asks. "Your horse phoned," replies his wife.

Don't accept rides from strange men and remember that all men are strange.

I like young girls. Their stories are shorter.

A daughter complains: "I can't stand it. All my husband wants is sex, sex, sex! My vagina used to be the size of a nickel. Now it's like a silver dollar!" Her mother says: "You live in a mansion, drive fancy cars, wear designer clothes! And you'd give all that up...over 95 cents?"

After church on Sunday, a man shook the minister's hand. "That was a damned fine sermon!" "Thank you, but I wish you wouldn't use profanity," said the pastor.
The man said, "I was so damned impressed that I put five thousand dollars in the offering plate." The preacher said, "No shit!"

At a party, a young lady teased the handsome, serious Marine. "You look very tense, Sergeant. How long since you had sex?" "1955, ma'am."
"Really! Well, let's go in that room over there and get you relaxed."
He quickly agreed. After several go-arounds, she said, "Wow, you sure didn't forget much since 1955!"
The Sergeant said, after glancing at his watch, "I hope not. It's only 21:30 now."

There was a bit of confusion in the market this morning. When I was ready to pay for my groceries, the cashier said, "$55.72. Strip down, please." I wasted no time in obeying her. When the hysterical shrieking finally subsided, I found out she was referring to my credit card. I have been asked to shop elsewhere in future.

There once was a man from McGill
Whose acts grew exceedingly ill.
He insisted on habits,
Involving white rabbits
And a bird with a flexible bill.

Warning signs that your lover is bored:
   1) Passionless kisses.
   2) Frequent sighing.
   3) Moved, left no forwarding address.
                              -Matt Groening

FEBRUARY STATISTICS ON AIRPORT SCREENING
Terrorists discovered 0
Transvestites............................. 133
Hernias 1,485
Hemorrhoid cases 3,177
Enlarged prostates 8,255
Breast implants 59,254
Natural blondes 3
It was also found that 535 politicians have no balls.

Q What do you get when you cross a penis with a totalitarian leader?
A A dick-tator

A man asked his doctor for a double dose of Viagra. "I'm sorry," said the doctor, "but that wouldn't be safe. Anyway, why do you need a double dose?"
"My girlfriend is coming to town on Friday, my ex-wife will be here Saturday, and my wife is coming home on Sunday. I really need it." The doctor finally agreed but told the man to come in on Monday for a checkup. He did, with his arm in a sling. The man explained, "No one showed up."

A young Chinese couple fall in love when she goes to work in his restaurant. They get married, both virgins.
On their wedding night, she undresses and gets into bed, terrified. He climbs in next to her and tries to be reassuring.
"My darling," he whispers. "I know this is your first time and you are very scared. I will do anything you want, anything. Just tell me what it is."
"Well..." she says after a silence. "I hear the girls talk about one thing all the time. I want us to try it."
"What is it, my love?"
"They call it Number sixty-nine."
"You want...garlic chicken with snow peas?"

JOAN RIVERS TALKS ABOUT SEX

A man can sleep around, no questions asked. But if a woman makes 19 or 20 mistakes, she's a tramp.

I spit on education. No man will ever put his hand up your dress looking for a library card.

A girl, you're 30 years old, you're not married—you're an old maid. A man, he's 90 years old, he's not married—he's a catch.

Gay marriage—I'm so against it, because all my gay friends are out and if they get married, it will cost me a fortune in gifts.

When you first get married, they open the car door for you. Eighteen years now ... once he opened the car door for me in the last four years...we were on the freeway at the time.

Don't talk to me about Valentine's Day. At my age, an affair of the heart is a bypass!

One more drink and I'll be under the host.

A woman was having a daytime affair while her husband was at work. One rainy day she was in bed with her boyfriend to her horror, she heard her husband's car come up the drive. "Hurry!" she exclaimed. "Grab your clothes and jump out the window...my husband's home early. If he finds you here, he'll kill us both.!" "But it's raining!"
"I'm telling you, if he finds us in bed, getting wet will be the least of your problems!"
So he scooted off the bed, grabbed his clothes and jumped out the window, running down the street in the pouring rain. He quickly discovered he had run into the middle of Seattle's Marathon. He joined them. After a short time, a runner who had spotted him with some curiosity, jogged closer. "Do you always run in the nude?"
"Oh yes!" he replied, a bit out of breath. "It feels so free!"
"And you always carry your clothes with you?" "Yes," he answered. "That way, I can get dressed right at the finish line, jump in my car, and go home."
The other runner's eyes lowered a bit. "And do you always wear a condom when you're running?"
"Only when it's raining."

The year is 2222 and Charlie and Marie land on Mars for a vacation. They meet a Martian couple and become quite friendly. Marie, who is very curious, finally gets up the nerve to ask how Martians make love. The Martian male says, "Pretty much the same way you do." A discussion ensues and pretty soon the couple agrees to swap partners.

Marie and the male Martian go off to a bedroom. They strip and she sees that he has a teeny weeny member. "I don't think this is going to work," says Marie. "Why not? What's the matter?"

"Well," she says, "it's not long enough to reach me." "No problem," he says, and proceeds to slap his forehead. With each slap his penis grows longer. "That's impressive," says Marie. "But it's very narrow." "No problem," he says and begins pulling his ears. With each pull, his penis becomes thicker. They fall onto the bed and make passionate love all night. The next day, the two couples meet up and go their separate ways. "I hate to say it," Marie says, "but it was wonderful. How about you?" "Horrible," says Charlie. "All I got was a headache. She kept slapping my forehead and pulling my ears."

An elderly man goes to the doctor, complaining that he hasn't peed in three weeks.
"How old are you?" asks the doctor.
"Ninety-three."
Says the doctor, "You've pee'd enough."

A man called his wife and said, "Honey, I've been invited to go fishing up in Canada with my boss. We'll be gone a week. Could you please pack enough clothes for a week and set out my rod and my fishing box. We're leaving from the office and I'll swing by the house to pick up my stuff.

"Oh, and please pack those new blue silk pj's."

The wife thought this fishing trip sounded a bit fishy but being a good wife, did as he asked.

The following week he returned home, looking tired but relaxed. His wife welcomed him home and asked if he'd caught any fish.

"Yes," he told her, "lots of bass, some bluegill, and even a swordfish...boy, that was some fight, landing him! But why didn't you pack my blue silk pj's like I asked?"

"Oh, but I did," she sweetly replied. "They're in your fishing box."

With Viagra such a hit, Pfizer is thinking about a whole new line of drug oriented toward improving the performance of men in today's society. For example:

DIRECTA – Just one dose given to men before leaving on car trips cause 72% of them to stop and ask directions when they got lost. Control group: 0.2%

PROJECTA – Men given this experimental new drug were far more likely to finish a household repair project before starting a new one.

COMPLIMENTRA – In clinical trials, 82% of middle-aged men given this drug noticed that their wives had a new hairstyle. The drug is currently being tested to see if its effects extend to noticing new clothing or new furniture.

BUYAGRA – Men given this drug reported sudden urges to buy the women in their lives expensive jewelry and other gifts, after only two days.

NEGA-VIAGRA – Has the exact opposite effect of Viagra; and is presently undergoing clinical trials on former United States presidents.

A gay guy who lived in Khartoum
Took a lesbian up to his room.
And they argued all night
Over who had the right
To do what, and with which, and to whom.

Two nuns came over from Scotland. One says to the other, "I hear they eat dogs here. Isn't that strange?"
"Odd, yes," says the other. "But if they eat dogs, we should at least try."
They go to a hotdog stand where one of the nuns says, "Two dogs, please."
"Sure thing," he says, "with mustard?"
"Oh yes, of course."
The vendor hands them the two hotdogs wrapped in foil.
The two nuns hurry to a nearby bench and begin to open the foil packets.
The first one to do so stares at it for a moment, then leans over to the other nun and whispers, "What part of the dog did YOU get?"

"George, you're too old to get married. Not only can't you cut the mustard, you can't even open the jar."
                    -LaWanda Page to George Burns

God said, "Adam, I have a good plan for you." And Adam said, "Whatever you say, I shall do." God said, "Go down into that valley." "Lord, what is a valley?"

God explained and then said, "Cross the river."

"Lord, what is a river?" God explained and then went on, "Go over to the hill..." "Lord, what is a hill?"

So God explained what a hill is. "And," he added, "on the other side of that hill, you will find a cave." "What is a cave?" Adam asked; and God explained. "In that cave there is a woman..."

"A woman?" So God explained what a woman is.

Then God said, "I want you to have sex with her so you can reproduce."

"How do I have sex?" asked Adam. God muttered, "Geez..." and then explained sex to Adam.

Adam then went down into the valley, across the river, over to the hill, and into the cave, and found the woman. In five minutes, he was back. God couldn't believe his eyes.

"Well??" he demanded.

And Adam said, "What's a headache?"

I think Philip Roth is a great writer.
> But I wouldn't want to shake his hand.
> -Jacqueline Susann

How lucky we are that we can reach our genitals instead of the spot on our back that itches.
> -Flash Rosenberg

Ignorance is bliss...but it'll never replace sex

A very shy guy goes into a bar and sees a lovely young woman sitting there alone. After many agonizing minutes of gathering courage, he goes up to her and quietly says, "Would you mind if we chatted for awhile?" She responds by loudly yelling, "NO, I WON'T SLEEP WITH YOU TONIGHT!" Everyone at the bar turns to stare. Naturally, he is totally humiliated and slinks back to his stool. After a few minutes, she walks over and says, "I'm so sorry if I embarrassed you. I'm a graduate student in psychology and I'm gathering information about how people respond to embarrassing situations."
To which he answers, at the top of his lungs: "WHAT DO YOU MEAN, $200?"

The Ultimate Bathroom Joke Book

Two guys in the woods. The first guy says, "Did you see that?" "No, what?"
"A bald eagle just flew overhead."
A few minutes later, the first guy cries, "Did you see that?" "No, what?"
"Are you blind? A big black bear was walking over that hill." After another minute or so: "Did you see _that_?"
"Yes," says the second guy with some belligerence. "Yes, I did."
"Then how come you stepped in it?"

There was a young fellow of Lyme
Who lived with three wives at one time.
When asked, "Why the third?"
He replied: "One's absurd,
And bigamy, sir, is a crime."

If businesses put their slogans on condom packages, you might see:
NIKE. Just Do It.
KFC. Finger Lickin' Good
BURGER KING. Have it Your Way
ENERGIZER. It keeps going and going
XBOX LIVE. It's good to play together.
HOME DEPOT. You can do it. We can help.
GATORADE. Is it in you?

She's the original good time had by all.

I had the competition in Trivia shot to pieces until the last question, which I got wrong.
The question was, Where do women have the curliest hair.
The correct answer, apparently, is Fiji.

A group of tough bikers were riding when they saw a girl about to jump off a bridge. The leader, a big burly man, gets off his bike and says, "What are you doing?"
"I'm going to commit suicide."
He says, "Before you jump, why don't you give me a kiss?"
She does, a long, deep, lingering kiss.
After she's done, the biker says, "Wow! That was the best kiss I have ever had. You really know what you're doing. And you're pretty, to boot. Why end your life?"
"My parents don't like me dressing up like a girl."

As a young doctor, pelvic exams on women embarrassed me and to cover up, I would whistle.
Once, the woman I was examining burst out laughing. It seems I was whistling "I wish I was an Oscar Meyer Wiener."

A man came into the ER yelling, "My wife's in labor and she's going to have the baby in the taxi!"
I was on duty.
I grabbed my gear and rushed out to the cab, lifted the lady's dress and began to remove her underwear, although she struggled quite a bit.
Suddenly I noticed there were several cabs. And I was in the wrong one.

Nadine and Steve were neighbors, and both loved gardening. Nadine couldn't help but notice that while her tomatoes were still a bit pink, Steve's were large and bright red.
"How do you get such beautiful fruit?" she asked him.
"Well, I come out in my bathrobe and flash the tomato plants and they turn red from blushing so much."
"I'll give it a try," said Nadine.
A few weeks later, Steve saw Nadine in the supermarket and said, "Well, how did you make out? Did it help with your tomatoes?"
"No," said Nadine, "but my cucumbers are enormous!"

A hard man is good to find.   -Mae West

The cardinal is doing a crossword puzzle. He asks the bishop, "What's a four-letter word for a female ending in _unt?"
Bishop: Aunt.
Cardinal: Can I borrow your eraser?

In Florida, a body is hurled from a fifth floor balcony. A neighbor rushes up to the apartment. "Mrs. Cohen, your husband just had a terrible accident. He fell from the balcony!"
She said, "That was no accident. I threw him off. I found him in bed with a 20-year-old. At his age, if he can screw, he can fly."

A young doctor made a house call on a new, rather elderly patient. "How long have you been bedridden?" he asked. After a confused silence, she said, "Not since my husband died."

A woman advertised for a man, who (1) doesn't beat women; (2) does not cheat with other women; and (3) is very good in bed. The next day, a man answers the ad and she notices he has no arms.
She: How do you qualify?
He: I rang the doorbell, didn't I?

Paddy comes into his favorite pub looking like he'd been in a train wreck. His face is bruised, his nose broken, and he's walking with a cane.
"What happened?" asked the bartender.
"Me and Jamie O'Connor had a big fight."
"Jamie O'Connor? That little punk? He must have had something in his hand."
"That he did," said Paddy. "A shovel is what had had and he gave me a terrible licking with it."
"You couldn't defend yourself? Didn't you have anything in your hand?"
"That I did," said Paddy.
"Mrs. O'Connor's breast... and a thing of beauty it was!"

A limerick's callous and crude,
With ideas distressingly lewd.
It's not worth the reading
By persons of breeding,
It's designed for us: vulgar and rude.

Many guys think the bigger a woman's breasts, the lower her I.Q. I don't think it works like that. I think it's the opposite. The bigger a woman's breasts, the lower a man's I.Q. becomes.

-Anita Wise

Tommy, 3 years old, is being toilet-trained but keeps missing the target. His mother, tired of always cleaning up after him, takes him to the pediatrician and tells the doctor the problem. Says the doctor, "His penis is a bit small. Undoubtedly it will grow, but in the meantime there's an old wive's tale that says if you give him two slice of toast each morning, it will grow nicely." The next morning, Tommy finds twelve slices of toast on the table. "Mommy!" he says, "That's too much. The doctor said two pieces."
"I know," says his mother. "The rest is for your Dad."

Young stud on the beach sees all the women crowding around an older man. "What's your secret?" he says.
"Stuff socks in your trunks," says the old guy.
Young guy does that and goes back to the beach. Nothing.
"Dummy!" says the old guy. "Stuff 'em in the FRONT."

What is a Yankee?
Same as a quickie but a guy can do it alone.

There's this young man, stranded on an island with only a Doberman and a pig for company. There's plenty of food and water and the weather is glorious, so everything is perfect except... no woman.

With every passing day, the pig looks better and better to him: smooth pink skin, lovely round posterior; but every time he makes a move toward the pig, the Doberman growls and shows his teeth in a very menacing way.

One day, a dinghy floats ashore and in the bottom of the little boat, all curled up and almost dead, is a lovely young woman.

The young man takes her into his shelter and slowly, slowly brings her back to life. When she is well enough to walk about and even take a little swim in the bay, she says to the young man, "I don't know how to thank you. I'll do anything you ask of me. Anything. Just name it."

The young man thinks for a minute and says,

"Would you mind taking the dog for a walk?"

Don't cook. Don't clean. No man ever desired a woman because she waxed the floor. "My God, the floor's immaculate! Lie down, you hot bitch."

-Joan Rivers

Gloria loves antique shops and one day she finds a particularly lovely mirror, which she takes home and shines up and puts it on the door of the bedroom she shares with her husband Marty.
One night, just for fun, she says, "Mirror, mirror on the door, make my breasts size 44," never thinking it might work.
There is a flash of light from the mirror and when she looks again, her breasts are indeed very large and firm.
She runs to tell her husband the good news and they both go back to the bedroom.
"Mirror, mirror on the door," Marty intones, "make my penis touch the floor."
Again, the bright flash of light...
And his legs fall off.

It seems I impregnated Marge,
So I do rather feel, by and large,
Some dough should be tendered
For services rendered.
But I can't quite decide what to charge.

When I was in labor, the nurses asked, "Do you still think blondes have more fun?"
                                      -Joan Rivers

A middle-aged couple with two beautiful daughters, decided to try one more time for a boy. Sure enough, the wife got pregnant and nine months later, delivered a healthy baby boy.
The joyful father rushed to the nursery and was horrified to see that his son was incredibly ugly.
He went to his wife and said, "I cannot possibly be the father of that hideous child. Look at the two beauties I fathered!"
Seeing his wife blush, he demanded, "Have you been fooling around on me?"
His wife confessed: "Not this time."

"I've got this thing for tall, lean men," said the new assistant at the software company. "That guy Mike in sales is certainly a long tall drink of water."
"I hate to bust your bubble, honey," replied the office veteran. "But, for a long tall drink of water, he's got an awfully short straw."

One of the side effects of Viagra is a headache.
Every time I take a pill, my wife gets a headache.

A new study says that having sex decreases your chances of catching a cold. The more sex you have, the less chance of getting a cold. Just wait 'til the guys get ahold of this. A woman will sneeze and he'll be saying, "Hey, I've got something for that!"

I recently picked a new primary care doctor. After exhaustive tests and two visits, he said I was doing pretty well for my age, which is 65. Pretty well? That didn't sound so good. "Do you think I'll reach 80?" I asked.
"Do you smoke, or drink?"
"Oh, no," I said, "and I don't do drugs, either."
"Do you eat steak and baby back ribs or pot roast or lamb chops?"
"No, my last doctor warned me off red meat."
"Do you spend a lot of time in the sun, swimming or boating or playing golf?" Again the answer was no. "Do you exercise or go biking or hiking?" "Not much," I said.
"Do you gamble, drive fast cars or have a lot of sexual activity?"
"No, not really," I said.
He studied me for a moment and said, "Then why do you give a shit?"

The day after the annual office Christmas party, Jim woke up with a pounding headache. Worse, he was unable to remember anything about the night before. After a trip to the bathroom and cold water splashed on his face, he gingerly made his way into the kitchen, where his wife gave him a cup of hot black coffee. "Louise," he moaned. "What happened last night? I can't remember a thing. Was it as bad as I think?" "Even worse," she assured him. "You made a complete ass of yourself, succeeding in antagonizing the entire board of directors; and then insulted your boss to his face."
"My boss! Who cares? He's an arrogant, self-important pig! Piss on him!"
"You did! All over his expensive suit," she informed him. "And he fired you."
"Well, screw him," said Jim.
"I did. You're back to work on Monday."

"Why did your boss jump out of the window?" "I don't know," the secretary sobbed. "He was so nice to me: diamond rings, fur coats...all kinds of presents. He asked me today how much it would cost to ravage me. I just said that the other men in the office always gave me fifty dollars."

The Ultimate Bathroom Joke Book

A man meets a gorgeous woman in a bar. They talk, they connect, and they end up leaving together.

They get back to her place and, as she shows him around, he notices that her bedroom is completed packed with teddy bears. Dozens of small bears are on a shelf a few inches from the floor, medium-sized ones are on a shelf a little higher, and very big bears are on the top shelf, against the wall. It's quite a collection but, okay, he figures she likes teddy bears, who cares?

She turns to him, then, they kiss, they kiss some more, they becomes excited, they take each other's clothes off and romp around for an hour or so. He's exhausted.

As they're lying on the bed together in the afterglow, he says, "So, baby, how'd I do?" She says, "You can have any prize from the bottom shelf."

What happens when you give Viagra to a lawyer? He grows taller.

Message from the hospital: Results from our lab test confirm that the red ring around your penis was not cancer. It was lipstick. Our sincere apologies for the amputation.

The Ultimate Bathroom Joke Book

A man is going to see a psychiatrist, who starts him off with Rorschach ink-blot tests. Every picture looks like a man and woman screwing to this patient.
The psychiatrist says, "It looks like you have a preoccupation with sex."
The man replies: "Well, you're the one with the dirty pictures."

Victoria's Secret and Smith & Wesson will merge and be called TittyTitty BangBang.

A bird was flying south for the winter but he was late and was frozen in a winter storm. He dropped down into a pasture where cows were grazing. There were cow pats all over the place, of course, and the frozen bird landed right in the middle of a big one. At first he was disgusted but then realized he was thawing out from the warmth and he cried out in joy. A nearby cat heard him and came to eat him.
There are three morals to this story:
1) Not everyone who gets you into shit is your enemy.
2) Not everyone who gets you out of shit is your friend.
3) If you find yourself in shit, keep your mouth shut.

Two lawyers are walking out of a restaurant and a beautiful young woman is walking by. One lawyer turns to his associate and comments, "Boy I'd love to screw her!"
The other attorney thinks for a second and then says, "Out of what?"

A man got a birthday present from his wife: a visit to a famous shaman living on a nearby reservation who was said to have a remedy for Erectile Dysfuntion.

He saw the shaman who handed him a small bottle. "This is powerful medicine," he warned, "and must be respected. Take only one teaspoonful and say, '1...2...3.' This will make you more potent than you have ever been in your life." The man said, "How do I stop the medicine from working?"

"Your partner must say '1...2...3...4.' And when she does, the medicine will not work again until the next full moon."

Eager to try this out, the man drove home and took his wife to the bedroom. They removed their clothes and he said "1...2...3." He was instantly aroused. His wife was also excited and said, "What's the 1...2...3 for?"

And that, boys and girls, is why we should never end a sentence with a preposition.

Three elderly ladies are sitting in the living room of their retirement home, talking about the things they liked to do when they were younger. The first old lady remembers her garden and how well her cucumber always did and she measures them out with her hands. The second old lady also recalls gardening and she shows with her hands how beautifully round her onions always grew. "I can't hear a word you're saying," said the third old lady, "But I certainly remember the man you're talking about."

Two older ladies meet for coffee one morning. Marge stared at the side of her friend's face and said, "Ilene, you have a suppository in your ear."
"Oh, God," said Ilene. "Now I know where the earpiece for my hearing aid is."

Statistics show that, by 70, there are five women to every man. Isn't that an ironic time for this to happen to a man.

Old age is when you know your way around but don't feel like going.

An 80 year old man is having his annual checkup. "I feel great," he tells his doctor. "And what's more, I've married again and my 30 year old wife is pregnant. How about that?" The doctor digests this information, and says, "I know a guy, an avid hunter. One day, he grabs his umbrella instead of his rifle and doesn't realize it. He meets a big bear and raises his umbrella and the bear drops dead in front of him, with a gunshot wound in his chest."
"But that's impossible," says the patient. "Someone else must have shot that bear."
Says the doctor: "Exactly."

A beloved pastor was leaving his congregation because he needed more money. When he told them, after the Sunday service, one by one, members got to their feet and offered a car, a larger house, education for the kids, life insurance...it went on and on. There was much applause. Then Agnes, aged 77, got to her feet and said, "If the pastor stays, I'll give him sex."
The pastor, blushing, asked whatever had possessed her to say such a thing.
"Well, I asked my husband what we could do to help, and he said, Screw him!"

Isaac and Sarah were married and went on their honeymoon.

When they got back, Sarah immediately phoned her mother, Lena.

"So?" said Lena. "How was the honeymoon, darling?" "Oh, it was wonderful, Mama. Fantastic! And so romantic! Suddenly, Sarah started to cry.

"Oh, Mama, as soon as we got back, Isaac started using such terrible language, language I had hoped never to hear! Please, Mama, come and get me. I don't want to be married!" Lena said, "Tell me, darling, what kind of language?" "Four-letter words, Mama! Come and get me now!" "Darling, tell your mother, don't be shy, tell me what four-letter words he used?"Sobbing, Sarah said:

"Cook. Wash. Dust."

Two men are arguing, leading to: 1) God bless Golda! 2) Screw Golda! 1) God bless Netenyahu! 2) Screw Bibi! 1) Are you Jewish? 2) No. Irish.

1) Well, screw Ella Fitzgerald!

A Florida couple, well in their 70s, goes to a sex therapist's office. They ask the therapist if he'll watch them as they have intercourse, to make sure they are doing it correctly.

The doctor is amazed at this suggestion, especially coming from such an elderly couple. But what could be the harm? He says okay.

When the couple finishes, he says, "There's absolutely nothing wrong with the way you make love." He thanks them for coming, charges them $50, and says goodbye.

To his astonishment, the next week they're back again, and with the same request.

Once again, he feels he cannot say no. They disrobe and commence their lovemaking. He thanks them for coming, charges them $50, and says goodbye.

When they come in a third time, he says he wants to know what's really going on.

"Well," says the guy, "Her husband is always home and my wife is always home. Motel 8 is $100, Embassy Suites is $250.

"When we come to you, it's $50, Medicaire pays 80% and AARP pays the rest.

"It's much cheaper!"

I had lunch with two of my unmarried girlfriends. One is engaged, one is a mistress, and me...well, I'm married for twenty years. We got to talking about men, then our relationships, and then our sex lives. Somehow we all decided to amaze our men by greeting them at the door wearing a black bra, stiletto heels and an eye mask, nothing else. We agreed to meet for lunch in a week and exchange notes.

    The engaged friend says: The other night when my boyfriend came over and found me in a black leather bodice, tall heels, and a mask, he said, "You are really something! I love you!" Then we made passionate love all night.

    The mistress says: I met my lover at his office and when I opened my raincoat to show him what I was wearing, he said not a word but grabbed me, threw me to the floor and we had wild sex right on the office carpet.

    Then I shared my story. When my husband came home, I was wearing the whole outfit, mask and all, standing there with my hip cocked. When he walked in the door and saw me, he grinned and said, "What's for dinner, Batman?"